Developing Web Applications with Oracle ADF Essentials

Quickly build attractive, user-friendly web applications using Oracle's free ADF Essentials toolkit

Sten E. Vesterli

BIRMINGHAM - MUMBAI

Developing Web Applications with Oracle ADF Essentials

Copyright © 2013 Packt Publishing

All rights reserved. No part of this book may be reproduced, stored in a retrieval system, or transmitted in any form or by any means, without the prior written permission of the publisher, except in the case of brief quotations embedded in critical articles or reviews.

Every effort has been made in the preparation of this book to ensure the accuracy of the information presented. However, the information contained in this book is sold without warranty, either express or implied. Neither the author nor Packt Publishing, and its dealers and distributors will be held liable for any damages caused or alleged to be caused directly or indirectly by this book.

Packt Publishing has endeavored to provide trademark information about all of the companies and products mentioned in this book by the appropriate use of capitals. However, Packt Publishing cannot guarantee the accuracy of this information.

First published: August 2013

Production Reference: 1160813

Published by Packt Publishing Ltd.
Livery Place
35 Livery Street
Birmingham B3 2PB, UK.

ISBN 978-1-78217-068-6

www.packtpub.com

Cover Image by Artie Ng (artherng@yahoo.com.au)

Credits

Author
Sten E. Vesterli

Reviewers
Eugene Fedorenko
Amr Gawish
Dimitrios Stasinopoulos

Acquisition Editors
Erol Staveley
Antony Lowe

Lead Technical Editor
Madhuja Chaudhari

Technical Editors
Anita Nayak
Pragati Singh
Vrinda Nitesh Bhosale

Project Coordinator
Apeksha Chitnis

Proofreader
Paul Hindle

Indexer
Hemangini Bari

Graphics
Ronak Dhruv

Production Coordinator
Aditi Gajjar

Cover Work
Aditi Gajjar

About the Author

Sten E. Vesterli picked up Oracle development as his first job after graduating from the Technical University of Denmark, and he hasn't looked back since. He has worked with almost every development tool and server Oracle has produced in the last two decades, including Oracle ADF, JDeveloper, WebLogic, SQL Developer, Oracle Portal, BPEL, Collaboration Suite, Designer, Forms, Reports, and even Oracle Power Objects.

He started sharing his knowledge with a conference presentation in 1997, and has since given more than 100 conference presentations at Oracle OpenWorld, ODTUG, IOUG, UKOUG, DOAG, and other user group conferences around the world. His presentations are highly rated by the participants, and in 2010, he received the ODTUG Best Speaker award.

He has also written numerous articles, participated in podcasts, and has written the books *Oracle Web Applications 101*, *The McGraw-Hill Companies* and *Oracle ADF Enterprise Application Development – Made Simple*, *Packt Publishing*. You can find his blog at `www.vesterli.com` and follow him on Twitter as `@stenvesterli`.

Oracle has recognized Sten's skills as an expert communicator on Oracle technology by awarding him the prestigious title of Oracle ACE Director, which is carried by less than 100 people in the world. He is also an Oracle Fusion User Experience Advocate and is a part of the Oracle Usability Advisory Board and participates in the Oracle WebLogic Partner Council.

Based in Denmark, Sten is a partner in the Oracle consulting company Scott/Tiger, where he works as a Senior Principal Consultant. When not writing books or presenting, he is helping customers choose the appropriate technology for their needs, teaching, mentoring, and leading development projects. In his spare time, Sten enjoys triathlons, and he completed his first Ironman in 2012.

Acknowledgement

As an ADF enthusiast, I'd like to thank Oracle for finally making a free version of Oracle ADF available. With it's high productivity and advanced features, ADF Essentials has the potential to become the standard way of writing data-handling applications. With this book, I hope to help that become a reality.

Others have gone before me in the quest to get the combination of ADF Essentials, MySQL, and GlassFish to work together. I'd especially like to thank Markus Eisele, Duncan Mills, Chris Muir, Jobinesh Purushothaman, Bauke Scholtz, and Shay Shmeltzer, whose work with ADF, Apache Shiro, MySQL, and GlassFish I have benefited from.

I also appreciate the efforts of the people at Packt Publishing who have been supporting this project, as well as my reviewers who have improved the book with their excellent questions and suggestions.

Finally, I'd like to thank my lovely wife for her love, support, and understanding for yet another book project.

About the Reviewers

Eugene Fedorenko is a senior analyst with extensive experience and management skills. He works for the Ukrainian software company CS Integra. The company focuses on banking software and is a leader in the local market. The company has been an Oracle Platinum partner since 2010 and it was rewarded as the Best Independent Software Vendor in the Eastern Europe region. Eugene graduated from the Kharkiv Aviation Institute in 1999 with an M.Sc. in Computer Science. He began his career in the company in 2000 as a developer. Currently, he is a senior analyst and he is in charge of running projects connected to Oracle Application Development Framework. He is the author of the ADF practice blog `http://adfpractice-fedor.blogspot.com` and a member of the ADF Enterprise Methodology Group.

Amr Gawish is a Senior Oracle Fusion Middleware Consultant. He is a certified WebCenter Portal and Oracle SOA implementation specialist. He has over five years of experience with the Oracle Middleware stack. He holds a Bachelor's degree in Math and Computer Sciences from Al-Azhar University in Egypt, and he has been involved in many ADF, WebCenter, and SOA projects. He currently works at infoMENTUM, which is an Oracle Gold Partner and a leading company in Oracle Fusion Middleware, and it is the first company to be specialized in WebCenter (both Content and Portal) in the EMEA region. It's what Amr calls "a place where innovation comes true!"

Amr is also currently authoring a book about ADF Faces called *Oracle ADF Faces Cookbook, Packt Publishing*.

> I'd like to thank my wife for helping and encouraging me to complete the review in time, and my daughter for always bringing a smile to my face.

Dimitrios Stasinopoulos is a Certified Application Development Framework Implementation Specialist with more than six years of experience in Oracle Fusion Middleware and, more specifically, in ADF BC 11*g*. Dimitrios currently works as an Oracle Fusion Middleware Consultant, mainly focusing on Oracle ADF, at e-DBA Ltd., an Oracle Platinum Partner. Dimitrios has worked in several Oracle ADF projects in various positions, from developer to architect, and he also enjoys teaching and talking about Fusion Middleware.

In his spare time, Dimitrios is helping the ADF community by answering technical questions in the Oracle ADF and JDeveloper forum, and he also maintains a blog where he posts his findings and ideas: `dstas.blogspot.com`.

Dimitrios holds a B.Sc. degree in Computer Science from the Technological Educational Institution of Larissa, Greece.

www.PacktPub.com

Support files, eBooks, discount offers and more

You might want to visit www.PacktPub.com for support files and downloads related to your book.

Did you know that Packt offers eBook versions of every book published, with PDF and ePub files available? You can upgrade to the eBook version at www.PacktPub.com and as a print book customer, you are entitled to a discount on the eBook copy. Get in touch with us at service@packtpub.com for more details.

At www.PacktPub.com, you can also read a collection of free technical articles, sign up for a range of free newsletters and receive exclusive discounts and offers on Packt books and eBooks.

http://PacktLib.PacktPub.com

Do you need instant solutions to your IT questions? PacktLib is Packt's online digital book library. Here, you can access, read and search across Packt's entire library of books.

Why Subscribe?

- Fully searchable across every book published by Packt
- Copy and paste, print and bookmark content
- On demand and accessible via web browser

Free Access for Packt account holders

If you have an account with Packt at www.PacktPub.com, you can use this to access PacktLib today and view nine entirely free books. Simply use your login credentials for immediate access.

Instant Updates on New Packt Books

Get notified! Find out when new books are published by following @PacktEnterprise on Twitter, or the *Packt Enterprise* Facebook page.

Table of Contents

Preface	**1**
Chapter 1: My First ADF Essentials Application	**9**
Getting ready	10
Installing MySQL	**10**
MySQL installation	12
Configuring	14
Changing MySQL options	16
Does it work?	16
Modifying some data	18
Installing Java Development Kit and GlassFish	**19**
Installing JDK 7	19
Installing GlassFish	21
GlassFish installation	22
Setting up the domain	23
Does it work?	24
Installing the MySQL connector in GlassFish	25
Adding a DataSource to GlassFish	25
Installing ADF Essentials	**27**
Getting ADF Essentials	27
Installing the ADF Share libraries in GlassFish	28
Setting the GlassFish JVM parameters	29
Does it work?	30
Installing JDeveloper	**30**
JDeveloper or Eclipse?	30
Which JDeveloper?	31
JDeveloper installation	32
Installing the MySQL Connector in JDeveloper	32
Installing the GlassFish Server Extension	33
Connecting to the GlassFish server	35

Building a simple ADF Essentials application	**36**
Creating the application	36
Database	38
Business service	38
Model layer	41
Controller layer	42
View layer	42
Getting ready to deploy	43
DataSource	44
Application module configuration	44
Change platform	44
Running your first ADF Essentials application	45
Can it run faster?	**47**
Setting up WebLogic for MySQL	47
Adding a DataSource to WebLogic	47
Running your first ADF Essentials application again	48
Summary	**48**
Chapter 2: Creating Business Services	**49**
Business service possibilities	**49**
ADF Business Components	**50**
Starting the example application	**53**
How ADF business components work	**53**
Building your own foundation	**56**
Building framework extension classes	57
Using framework extension classes	58
Building entity objects for the example application	**59**
Preparing to build	60
Running the wizard	61
Examining the result	62
Setting the labels	63
Autogenerated values	63
Cleaning up the data types	64
Cleaning up the associations	66
Deleting superfluous associations	67
Fixing wrong associations	68
Removing invalid references from entity objects	70
Building view objects	**71**
The storyboard	71
Building the customer view object	72
Building the rental view object	75
Creating a view link	78
Application module	**79**

Testing business components	82
Summary	83
Chapter 3: Creating Task Flows and Pages	**85**
Building task flows	86
Bounded and unbounded task flows	86
Pages and fragments	87
Task flow templates	88
Example application	89
Building the Rent DVD task flow	89
Building the Return DVD task flow	92
Memory scopes	97
Other elements of task flows	98
Building pages	99
Using templates	99
Facet definitions	100
Page fragment template	100
Page template	102
Example application	106
Building the customer search page	106
Building the Return DVD page	109
An alternative – ADF query panel	109
Building the Rent DVD page	109
Building a master page	110
Running the page	112
Using data bindings	113
Showing a customer on a page	113
Showing customer rentals on a page	116
Adding navigation	120
Summary	120
Chapter 4: Adding Business Logic	**121**
Adding logic to business components	121
Logic in entity objects	122
Overriding accessors	122
Working with database triggers	124
Overriding doDML()	125
Data validation	127
Declarative validation	127
Regular expression validation	129
Groovy scripts	130
Method validation	130
Logic in view objects	130
Overriding accessors	131
Change view criteria	132
Logic in application modules	134

Adding logic to the user interface — 135
Adding a bean method to a button — 135
Adding a bean to a task flow — 136
Accessing UI components from beans — 137
Accessing the binding layer — 138
Working with attribute values — 138
Working with operations — 139
Working with whole datasets — 140
Showing messages — 140
Example application — 141
Registering a rental — 142
Creating a bean — 142
Mapping the fields — 143
Establishing bindings — 144
Writing the code — 146
Registering a return — 147
Adding a column and a button — 147
Creating a bean — 148
Mapping the table — 148
Creating a view object method — 149
Publishing your method — 150
Establishing bindings — 151
Writing the bean code — 151
Marking items returned today — 152
Creating a transient attribute — 152
Binding the new attribute — 153
Coding the attribute return value — 153
Using the attribute value — 154
Other ideas — 155
Summary — 155

Chapter 5: Building Enterprise Applications — 157
Structuring your code — 157
Workspaces and projects — 158
The workspace hierarchy — 158
The directory structure — 159
Using version control — 160
Working with ADF libraries — 162
Creating ADF libraries — 162
Releasing ADF libraries — 163
Using ADF libraries — 164
Example application — 164
Creating the Master Application Workspace — 165
Creating the workspace — 165

Adding to source control	166
Creating the ADF library folder	168
Creating the CommonCode workspace	**169**
Creating the workspace	169
Recreating the framework extension classes	169
Check your JDeveloper preferences	170
Adding to source control	170
Creating the ADF library	171
Releasing the ADF library	172
Creating the CommonUI workspace	**172**
Creating the workspace	172
Creating the templates	172
Adding an ADF library	174
Adding to source control	175
Creating and releasing the ADF library	175
Creating the CommonModel workspace	**176**
Creating the workspace	176
Adding an ADF library	176
Creating the entity objects	176
Adding to source control and creating the ADF library	177
Creating the RentDvd subsystem workspace	**178**
Creating the workspace	178
Adding ADF libraries	178
Creating the view object	179
Creating the application module	180
Creating the task flow and page fragment	181
Adding a binding	181
Adding the business logic	182
Remaining work	182
Creating the ReturnDvd subsystem workspace	**182**
Creating the workspace	183
Adding ADF libraries	183
Creating the Customer view object	183
Creating the Rental view object	184
Creating a View Link	185
Creating an application module	185
Creating the task flow	187
Creating the Customer Search Page Fragment	187
Creating the Rentals Page Fragment	188
Registering a return	188
Remaining work	188
Finishing the Master Application Workspace	**189**
Adding the ADF libraries	189
Create the master page	189
Summary	**190**

Table of Contents

Chapter 6 Debugging ADF Applications	**191**
ADF logging	**191**
Creating a logger	192
Adding log statements	192
Business logging	194
JDeveloper shortcuts	194
Reading the logs	197
Logging in GlassFish	**199**
Controlling domain logging	200
Controlling individual loggers	200
Debugging in JDeveloper	**201**
Debugging code	201
Understanding the ADF lifecycle	203
Debugging task flows	204
Debugging into ADF libraries	206
Creating a source directory	206
Creating a source JAR file	207
Including the source in the master application	208
Placing a breakpoint in an ADF library	208
Debugging into the ADF source code	210
Summary	**211**
Chapter 7: Securing an ADF Essentials Application	**213**
Apache Shiro basics	**213**
Getting the software	214
Installing the packages in your application	214
Configuring your application for Shiro	216
Advanced Shiro	**217**
User database	218
Form-based authentication	219
The login page	220
The login bean	220
The login method	221
The user filter	222
The Shiro configuration	223
Accessing the user	224
Implementing authorization	**225**
Can I see some ID, please?	225
Are you a member, Sir?	225
Disabling elements	226
Removing elements	227
Securing task flows	227
Summary	**228**

Chapter 8: Build and Deploy — 229
Creating a build script — 229
Creating the script — 231
Deploying a single application — 232
Building the master application — 233
Starting point — 233
Building the application EAR file — 234
Building all the subsystems — 235
Copying all ADF libraries — 236
Putting it all together — 237
Automated deployment to GlassFish — 237
Deploying from the command line — 238
Deploying from Ant — 238
Integrating other functionality in your build — 239
Preparing to go live — 239
Cleaning up your code — 239
Database connections — 240
Deployment platforms — 241
Print statements — 242
Tuning your ADF application — 242
Summary — 242
Index — 243

Preface

Oracle ADF is the most productive framework available today for building data-handling web applications. With just a little training (like you can get from this book), you will be able to build fully-functional applications to meet a wide variety of needs.

Until September 2012, this powerful tool was reserved for organizations and projects able to pay for an Oracle WebLogic Server license, which is not quite cheap. But that month, after years of badgering by ADF enthusiasts, Oracle finally decided to make a free, slightly limited version of Oracle ADF available to everyone.

This means the fastest, easiest, and cheapest way of building a data-handling application today is with the technology stack described in this book:

- The free MySQL database
- The free GlassFish application server
- The free ADF Essentials toolkit
- The free JDeveloper development tool

The prescription

When pharmaceutical companies develop drugs, they are targeting specific ailments or situations. Similarly, IT development platforms and frameworks target specific use cases. And the "sweet spot" for the ADF framework is data-handling applications.

What is a data-handling application? It is an application whose primary function is to gather data, process them, and display them back to the user as tables or graphs. Examples of data-handling applications are membership databases, project and task management, or accounting programs.

With very powerful declarative features, you can build most of your application without having to write any code, and the advanced user interface components make it easy to build an attractive user interface including interactive graphical displays of your data.

Off-label use

After release, some drugs are found to be potentially useful for other conditions than those for which they were developed and tested. This is called "off-label use" — using the drug for something that it was not intended for.

A similar situation occurs in the development of IT systems -- developers choose a tool that is a brilliant choice for one type of applications and try to use it for other types.

The classic case of "off-label use" of ADF is to build an application where you require absolute control over every pixel and every interaction. Such control is often possible to achieve with ADF, but it takes a big effort and requires deep modifications to the core of the framework.

Allergies

In medicine, some people are allergic to certain medicines and should not be given them.

Similarly, there are some types of highly interactive applications like games or photo editing that are definitely unsuited for ADF.

What's not there

ADF Essentials contains everything you need to build a data-handling application -- but of course, there has to be some additional features only available to enterprise customers with a full ADF license.

Some of the things not included in ADF Essentials include ADF Mobile, ADF Security (which is based on Oracle Platform Security Services, available only in WebLogic), Web Service Data Controls, ADF Desktop Integration, and so on. Refer to the ADF Essentials "Frequently Asked Questions" document for the full list.

However, it is worth repeating that everything you need in order to build data-handling applications is there. Actually, everything is there -- the restriction is only a legal and licensing issue.

The sample application

Throughout this book, a sample application for a DVD rental shop is built. You can follow along in JDeveloper as you read, learning ADF hands-on.

The data model is the standard `sakila` database schema that comes with MySQL. The part we use consists of the `customer`, `film`, `inventory`, and `rental` tables -- their relationship looks as shown in the following diagram:

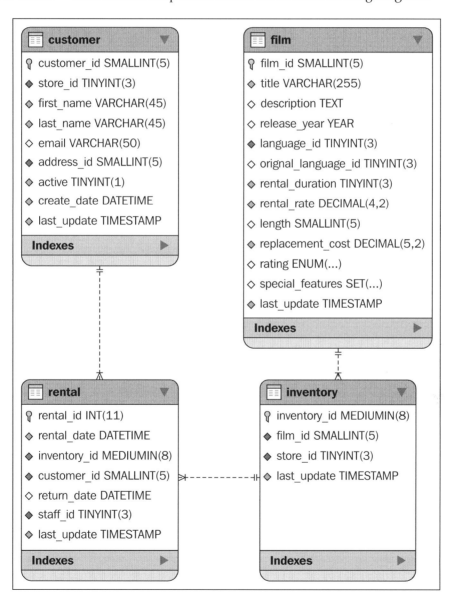

Preface

We will build three application screens: one simple screen for registering a rental, and two connected screens for searching for a customer and registering a return. These two screens look as shown in the following diagram:

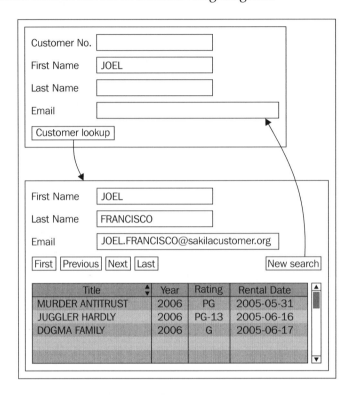

What this book covers

Chapter 1, My First ADF Essentials Application, shows you how to install all the software and build a very simple application to prove that everything works.

Chapter 2, Creating Business Services, describes what Business Components are and how they are used in the example application. No code required!

Chapter 3, Creating Task Flows and Pages, shows you how to build ADF task flows that control the flow of your application and how to build the ADF pages where the user interacts with the data. Still no code required!

Chapter 4, Adding Business Logic, explains how to add business logic to your application -- this is where you'll have to write some actual Java code to implement functionality that ADF does not offer declaratively.

Chapter 5, *Building Enterprise Applications*, demonstrates how you go about building a larger application, using subsystems and ADF libraries to divide a big application into more manageable parts. We'll quickly build the whole DVD rental application again in this chapter using proper enterprise methodology.

Chapter 6, *Debugging ADF Applications*, shows you how to use ADF logging and debugging features to troubleshoot any problems you might experience during your ADF development.

Chapter 7, *Securing an ADF Essentials Application*, implements Apache Shiro to secure your application. Remember that there were some ADF-specific security features not part of ADF Essentials? This chapter shows you a fully-functional alternative.

Chapter 8, *Build and Deploy*, demonstrates how to use Apache Ant to create build scripts that compile, build, and deploy an entire enterprise application, including subsystems and ADF libraries.

What you need for this book

This book uses the following software:

- MySQL database version 5.6
- GlassFish application server 3.1
- ADF Essentials 11.1.2.4
- JDeveloper 11.1.2.4

Chapter 1, *My First ADF Essentials Application*, explains where to get the software, how to install it, and how to configure all the parts to work together.

Who this book is for

This book is for every web developer who wants to build data-handling applications quickly and efficiently. The book does not require any preconditions -- even beginners can use the powerful declarative features of ADF to build basic applications completely without programming.

Most real-life applications will of course require some programming to implement the business logic that is specific to your application. ADF uses Java to implement business logic, so a basic understanding of Java programming is required for most applications. A bit of knowledge about web applications in general will also be beneficial.

Preface

Conventions

In this book, you will find a number of styles of text that distinguish between different kinds of information. Here are some examples of these styles, and an explanation of their meaning.

Code words in text, database table names, folder names, filenames, file extensions, pathnames, dummy URLs, user input, and Twitter handles are shown as follows: "Just like a SELECT statement can join data from multiple tables, a view object can join data from multiple entity objects".

A block of code is set as follows:

```
protected void doDML(int operation, TransactionEvent e) {
  super.doDML(operation, e);
}
```

When we wish to draw your attention to a particular part of a code block, the relevant lines or items are set in bold:

```
if (operation == DML_INSERT) {
  String insStmt = "{call insertActor (?,?)}";
  cstmt = getDBTransaction().createCallableStatement(insStmt,
    0);
  try {
    cstmt.setString(1, getFirstName());
    cstmt.setString(2, getLastName());
    cstmt.execute();
  }
  catch (Exception ex) {
    ...
  }
}
```

New terms and **important words** are shown in bold. Words that you see on the screen, in menus or dialog boxes for example, appear in the text like this: "clicking on the **Next** button moves you to the next screen".

> Warnings or important notes appear in a box like this.

> Tips and tricks appear like this.

Reader feedback

Feedback from our readers is always welcome. Let us know what you think about this book—what you liked or may have disliked. Reader feedback is important for us to develop titles that you really get the most out of.

To send us general feedback, simply send an e-mail to feedback@packtpub.com, and mention the book title via the subject of your message.

If there is a topic that you have expertise in and you are interested in either writing or contributing to a book, see our author guide on www.packtpub.com/authors.

Customer support

Now that you are the proud owner of a Packt book, we have a number of things to help you to get the most from your purchase.

Errata

Although we have taken every care to ensure the accuracy of our content, mistakes do happen. If you find a mistake in one of our books—maybe a mistake in the text or the code—we would be grateful if you would report this to us. By doing so, you can save other readers from frustration and help us improve subsequent versions of this book. If you find any errata, please report them by visiting http://www.packtpub.com/submit-errata, selecting your book, clicking on the **errata submission form** link, and entering the details of your errata. Once your errata are verified, your submission will be accepted and the errata will be uploaded on our website, or added to any list of existing errata, under the Errata section of that title. Any existing errata can be viewed by selecting your title from http://www.packtpub.com/support.

Piracy

Piracy of copyright material on the Internet is an ongoing problem across all media. At Packt, we take the protection of our copyright and licenses very seriously. If you come across any illegal copies of our works, in any form, on the Internet, please provide us with the location address or website name immediately so that we can pursue a remedy.

Please contact us at `copyright@packtpub.com` with a link to the suspected pirated material.

We appreciate your help in protecting our authors, and our ability to bring you valuable content.

Questions

You can contact us at `questions@packtpub.com` if you are having a problem with any aspect of the book, and we will do our best to address it.

1
My First ADF Essentials Application

In this chapter, we will install all the necessary (free!) software that we will be using throughout the book to build applications using Oracle **Application Development Framework** (**ADF**). We'll need:

- A database
- Java Development Kit and an application server
- The Oracle ADF Essentials libraries
- A development tool

For the purposes of this book, we will be using the popular and free MySQL database. However, you can run Oracle ADF Essentials applications on any other SQL database — so if you're a PostgreSQL fan, you don't have to change. You can also use commercial databases — Oracle is offering Oracle Database Express Edition if you are looking for a free version of an enterprise product.

> Don't plan on running Oracle Database Express Edition directly on your development machine if it is 64-bit Windows — this is not supported and won't work. To run Oracle XE, you'll either need Linux, an old 32-bit Windows install, or run your database inside a 32-bit Windows virtual machine.

Similarly, you can run your ADF Essentials application on any JEE application server. This book will describe how to use GlassFish, but you could also use other open source JEE servers like JBoss or commercial offerings like Oracle WebLogic.

My First ADF Essentials Application

As our development tool, we will be using Oracle's preferred development tool, Oracle JDeveloper. This free tool is currently the only supported way of building Oracle ADF Essentials applications, but Oracle is working on supporting ADF Essentials as part of their Oracle Enterprise Pack for Eclipse (OEPE) product.

> With Eclipse and Oracle Enterprise Pack for Eclipse, you can already build ADF applications for WebLogic. However, the tool does not yet support building applications for ADF Essentials.

Getting ready

To simplify the instructions in this book, you should create a directory called `adfessentials` and install everything there.

On Windows, place this directory in the root of your C: drive as `C:\adfessentials`.

On Mac/Linux, place this directory in the root of your filesystem as `/adfessentials`. You will typically be prompted for a system administrator or root password when creating the directory.

Installing MySQL

The MySQL server exists in both a Community Server edition and an Enterprise Edition. The Enterprise Edition is the commercial version that has additional features and a price tag—in this book, we will use the free Community Server edition Version 5.6.12. This can be downloaded from `http://dev.mysql.com/downloads/mysql`.

> **Would you like support with that?**
>
> Now is a good time to think about whether you want your installation to be commercially supported. If you are setting up a development environment or just want to run a membership application for your local little league baseball team, you probably don't need commercial support and can go with the open source/community options.
>
> On the other hand, if you are setting up a production environment, think about whether you or someone else in your organization feels confident that they can handle any issues that might occur. If you would like to be able to call on the friendly people from Oracle Support to help you, you need to set up the commercial version and purchase a support contract from Oracle.

If you choose the Windows platform, you will be given the option to download the MySQL Installer MSI package as shown in the following screenshot:

When you click on the **Download** link, you will be taken to a page where you can select from two **MSI Installer** packages as shown in the following screenshot:

Choose the larger one to get everything in one download. The smaller option means that you download only the installer program first, and this program will then download the rest of the software.

My First ADF Essentials Application

If you are running Mac OS X, you have an option to select either a compressed TAR file or a DMG installer as shown in the following screenshot:

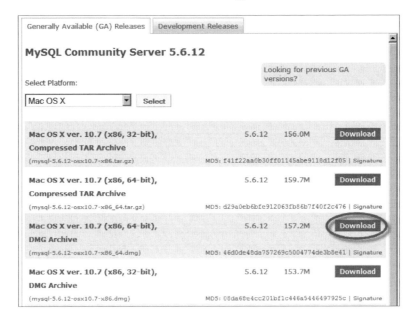

For the easiest installation, choose the DMG installer file that matches your OS X version and architecture. If you have a fairly recent Mac, you should choose OS X 10.7, 64-bit.

If you are running Linux, choose your distribution from the **Platform** options (or **Linux – Generic** if your distribution is not listed), and then choose the download that matches your Linux version and architecture (32- or 64-bit).

Once you have chosen your download, you will be prompted to sign up for a free Oracle Web account (or log in with an existing account) when you click on the **Download** link. You will need this account in order to download the ADF Essentials software and JDeveloper, and probably later for other downloads as well.

MySQL installation

This section will walk you through the installation of the MySQL database on Windows – if you are running another operating system, the process is similar.

 Some installation options of some Linux distributions install MySQL by default. If you are running Linux, you might want to check if you already have MySQL.

Start the installer, click on OK to any warnings about installing software and changing your machine, and choose **Install MySQL Products**. Read and accept the license agreement and allow it to check for later versions of the software.

For the purposes of this book, you can simply choose a **Developer Default** setup type when prompted. If you already know MySQL and have specific ideas about your installation, feel free to change the options.

Change the installation path to `C:\adfessentials\MySQL\product` and the data path to `C:\adfessentials\MySQL\data`.

> On Mac and Linux, the installer might simply decide to place the software and data in `/usr/local`. That's fine, too.

In the **Check Requirements** step, you may be prompted to install various additional packages — simply accept this. If you are told that you are missing various versions of the Python programming language, you can just click on Execute a few times to acknowledge the warnings.

> The **Developer Default** installation includes database connectors for Python, but if you are not using Python, they can't be installed. That's OK.

Once you are done with this step, the installer starts installing the actual MySQL software as shown as follows:

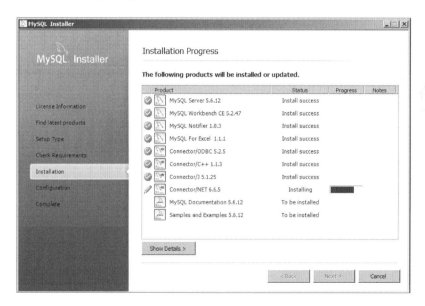

Configuring

When the software is installed, you can click on **Next** a few times to start the configuration. The first screen looks like this:

On this screen, you can leave the defaults:

- Development Machine
- Enable TCP/IP
- Port Number 3306
- Open Firewall for network access

In step 2 shown in the following screenshot, you are asked to provide a root password for the database. You can always create separate users later.

> If this is a non-critical development workstation, and you want to be sure that you have the password written down, feel free to use this example password: `ADFsecret/13`.

Chapter 1

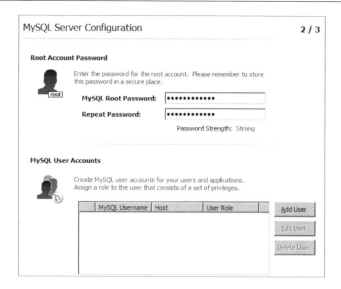

 The default installation on Mac and Linux sets a blank root password, which is probably a bit too relaxed. To set the password on Mac/Linux, execute the following command:

`/usr/local/mysql/bin/mysqladmin -u root -p password`

Press return when prompted for a password (the prompt is for the old, empty password) and then provide a new password twice.

In step 3, you are prompted for a Windows service name as shown in the following screenshot:

My First ADF Essentials Application

You can leave the defaults on this screen.

When you click on **Next**, the configuration of MySQL runs. When this is complete, click on **Next** to install the samples and examples and then finish the installation.

Changing MySQL options

JDeveloper generates code with two vertical bars (|| or pipes) for string concatenation, and while this is valid SQL92, it is not supported in a default MySQL configuration. To enable this in MySQL, find the MySQL configuration file my.ini in the database directory (for example, C:\adfessentials\MySQL\data).

Search for a line starting with sql_mode=. If such a line exists, add a comma after the existing value and then the keyword PIPES_AS_CONCAT. If there is no sql_mode line, add the following:

```
sql_mode=PIPES_AS_CONCAT
```

If you come from an Oracle background, you might want to set sql_mode=ORACLE instead—this sets PIPES_AS_CONCAT and a couple of other settings to make MySQL behave more Oracle-like.

You will need to restart the MySQL database in order for this change to take effect. On Windows, you can open the **Control Panel**, choose **Administrative Tools**, and then **Services**. Find the **MySQL56** service and choose **Action | Restart**. You can also restart the database from the **MySQL Workbench** by double-clicking on your database in the **Server Administration** column to the right.

Does it work?

Once you have your Sakila database installed, you can start the MySQL Workbench from the **Start** menu. You should see **Local instance MySQL56** or similar to the left under the **SQL Development** heading, as shown in the following screenshot:

You can double-click on this and provide your root password to connect to the database. If an **SQL Editor** window opens with various schemas to the left (including your Sakila database) as shown in the following screenshot, your installation was successful:

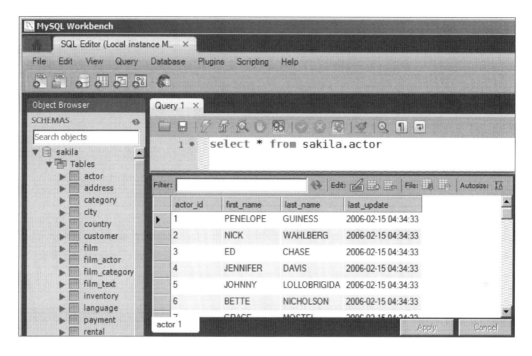

If you prefer to use a command line, you can start the MySQL 5.6 Command Line Client from the **Start** menu, provide your root password, and type the following command:

`show databases;`

My First ADF Essentials Application

If you see a couple of databases as in the following screenshot, your MySQL server is running correctly:

The MySQL command line can also be started from a command prompt by running the following command:

`C:\adfessentials\MySQL\product\bin\mysql -u root -p`

This attempts to log in as user `root` and prompts you for the password.

> On Mac and Linux, the MySQL Workbench is a separate package. You can either download and install it or check your installation using the command line:
>
> `/usr/local/mysql/bin/mysql -u root -p`

Modifying some data

As installed, the Sakila database does not contain any DVDs not returned—every `rental` record has a `return_date`.

Because we will be building a screen to return DVDs, we want some unreturned rentals in the database. From either MySQL Workbench or the command line, execute the following command:

```
update rental set return_date = null where staff_id = 2;
```

This clears the return date for about half the rentals, making them unreturned.

Installing Java Development Kit and GlassFish

In order to be able to install and run GlassFish, your system first needs to have JDK 7 installed.

Installing JDK 7

You can download Java Development Kit 7 from `http://www.oracle.com/technetwork/java/javase/downloads`. You need the JDK download as shown in the following screenshot:

Accept the license agreement and choose the right bundle for your operating system and architecture, for example, Windows x64 for 64-bit Windows or Windows x86 for 32-bit Windows.

My First ADF Essentials Application

When the installation is complete, double-click on the downloaded file to install the JDK. In the second step of the install wizard, change the directory to one placed under your `adfessentials` folder, for example, `C:\adfessentials\jdk1.7.0_25` as shown in the following screenshot:

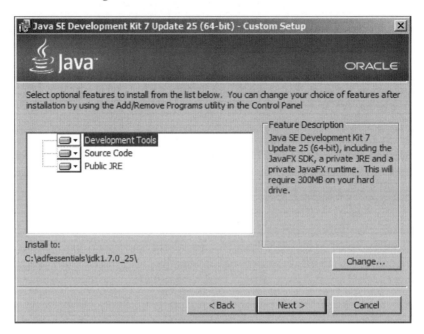

When asked where to install the JRE, change the destination folder to `C:\adfessentials\jre7` as shown in the following screenshot:

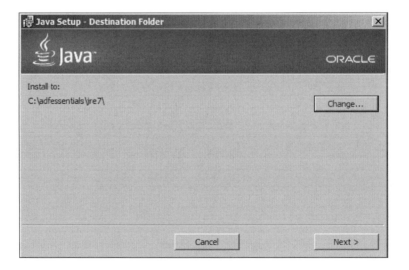

When the installation is complete, you need to set your `JAVA_HOME` environment variable to point to the JDK directory (for example, `C:\adfessentials\jdk1.7.0_25`).

Installing GlassFish

> At the time of writing, Version 4.0 of GlassFish has been released, but you cannot run ADF Essentials on it. So, this book will concentrate on GlassFish 3.1.

GlassFish Server Open Source Edition 3.1.2.2 can be downloaded from `http://glassfish.java.net/download-archive.html`. Like MySQL, GlassFish exists in both an open source version and a commerical version – if you want the commercial version, it can be found on the Oracle Technology Network under Middleware, GlassFish Server.

As the following screenshot shows, there are install sets available for Windows, Linux, Unix, Mac, and so on. Just click on the link for the file that matches your environment:

GlassFish - World's first Java EE 7 Application Server

Archived Releases

GlassFish Server Open Source Edition 3.1.2.2 (Java EE 6)

Platform	Java EE 6	Locale	
Windows	Web Profile	EN	glassfish-3.1.2.2-web-windows.exe
	Full Platform	EN	glassfish-3.1.2.2-windows.exe
Windows	Web Profile	ML	glassfish-3.1.2.2-web-windows-ml.exe
	Full Platform	ML	glassfish-3.1.2.2-windows-ml.exe
Linux, Mac, Solaris	Web Profile	EN	glassfish-3.1.2.2-web-unix.sh
	Full Platform	EN	glassfish-3.1.2.2-unix.sh
Linux, Mac, Solaris	Web Profile	ML	glassfish-3.1.2.2-web-unix-ml.sh
	Full Platform	ML	glassfish-3.1.2.2-unix-ml.sh

GlassFish installation

To install GlassFish, change to the directory where you downloaded the file and execute the following command:

`glassfish-3.1.2.2-windows.exe -j c:\adfessentials\jdk1.7.0_25`

 [The GlassFish installation file sometimes cannot find your Java Development Kit, especially on 64-bit Windows. The preceding command works in all environments.]

In the GlassFish installer, choose the following options:

- **Installation type**: Typical
- **Install directory**: `c:\adfessentials\glassfish3`
- **Update tool**: Don't choose this

 [You do not want your server to automatically update itself. If one of your applications is not compatible with the new server version, your users will experience that the application is suddenly down, and you will have no idea that it has happened until they tell you.]

- The installer runs and installs the GlassFish software shown as follows:

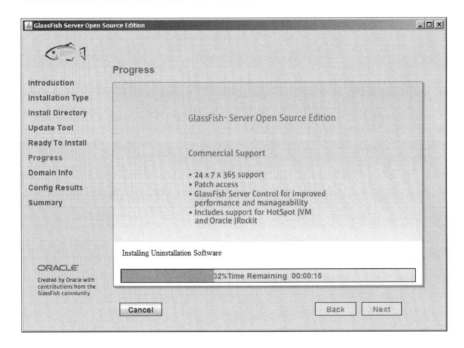

Setting up the domain

When the software is installed, the installer will prompt you to create a domain like this:

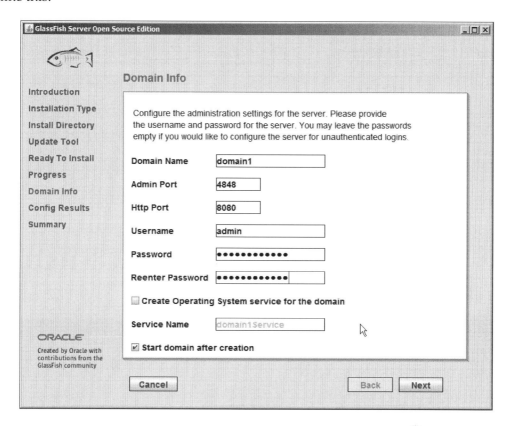

You can leave the default domain name and ports. You should set a password for the admin user—again, if this is a non-critical development workstation and you want to be sure that you have the password written down, feel free to use this example password: ADFsecret/13.

> If you are already running an Oracle database on the same machine, change the default HTTP port to something other than the default 8080 (because an Oracle database by default installs a service on port 8080).

After the domain has been created and started, click on **Next** to see the installation summary as shown in the following screenshot:

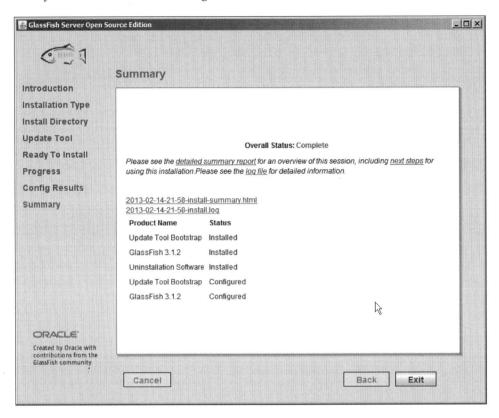

When you click on **Exit**, you will be prompted to register your GlassFish server, but this is not mandatory.

Does it work?

In order to check if your GlassFish server is indeed running, you can enter the URL `http://localhost:<port>` (for example, `http://localhost:8080`) in your browser to see the **Your server is now running** confirmation message like this:

Installing the MySQL connector in GlassFish

In order to be able to connect from GlassFish to a database, you need a connector. GlassFish does not have a MySQL connector built-in, so you need to go to http://www.mysql.com/products/connector and download the **JDBC Connector for MySQL (Connector/J)**. You may be prompted to log on to your Oracle Web account.

Unpack the file and copy the mysql-connector-java-5.1.25-bin.jar file (or whatever the version number is by the time you read this) into the lib directory of your GlassFish domain (C:\adfessentials\glassfish3\ glassfish\domains\ domain1\lib or similar). Then, stop GlassFish and start it again (on Windows, the start and stop commands are found on the **Start** menu under **GlassFish Server Open Source Edition**).

Adding a DataSource to GlassFish

In order for your applications to be able to connect to your MySQL database, you need to define a DataSource. Your applications will refer to the DataSource by name, and the configuration on the GlassFish server defines which database the DataSource will connect to. This gives the application server administrator the necessary freedom to move the application between environments, move databases to other servers, and so on.

My First ADF Essentials Application

You can set up a DataSource though the GlassFish Server Administration Console. You specified the port for this service as the Admin port when you installed GlassFish. The default port is 4848, so you can point your browser to `http://localhost:4848` to start the admin console.

Open the **Resources** node on the left and then **JDBC**. Click on **JDBC Connection Pools** and then click on **New** in order to create a new connection pool. Give it the name `SakilaPool`, choose **javax.sql.DataSource** as **Resource Type**, and choose **MySql** as **Database Driver Vendor**. Your screen should look like this:

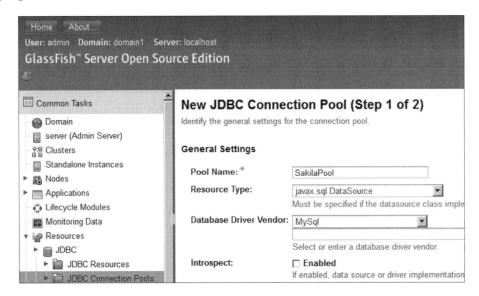

On the next screen, scroll down to the **Additional Properties** section and sort the properties by name (by clicking in the **Name** header). Find the following settings and set their value as follows:

- **databaseName**: sakila
- **password**: `ADFsecret/13` (or whatever other password you chose when you installed MySQL)
- **servername**: `localhost`
- **user**: `root`

When you have clicked on **Finish** to create the pool, click on the **SakilaPool** name and then click on the **Ping** button to test that GlassFish can connect to MySQL. You should see a **Ping Succeded** message as shown in the following screenshot:

Chapter 1

Then, click on **JDBC Resources** and then click on **New** in order to create a new JDBC resource. Give it the JNDI name `jdbc/SakilaDS` and select the **SakilaPool** connection pool for this JDBC resource as shown in the following screenshot:

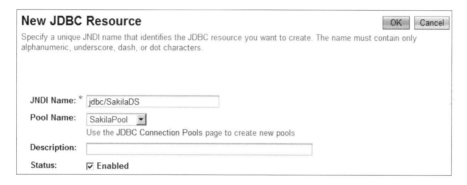

Installing ADF Essentials

In order to run ADF Essentials applications in GlassFish, you will need to install the ADF Share libraries in your GlassFish domain and you will need to configure the GlassFish Server JVM memory parameters.

Getting ADF Essentials

You can get the ADF Essentials package from the Oracle Technology Network—at the time of writing, the download URL is `http://www.oracle.com/technetwork/developer-tools/adf/downloads`. If this does not work, you can get to the Downloads for Oracle ADF 11*g* page by starting at the OTN homepage (`http://otn.oracle.com`), clicking **Software downloads** to the left, then scrolling down and clicking on **JDeveloper and ADF**, then selecting **Application Development Framework** to the left, and finally clicking on the **Downloads** tab.

[27]

My First ADF Essentials Application

The download page will look something like this:

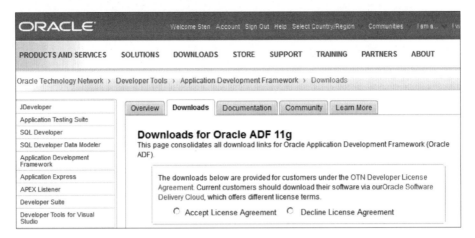

Accept the license agreement (read it first!) and then scroll down to the Oracle ADF Essentials section shown in the following screenshot and download:

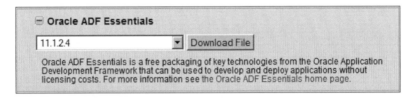

You may be asked to fill in a short survey before Oracle lets you have the software, and you'll probably be asked to accept the license agreement once more — just to be on the safe side.

The download you get is the `adf-essentials.zip` file.

Installing the ADF Share libraries in GlassFish

To install the ADF Share libraries in GlassFish, first unpack your `adf-essentials.zip` file in a temporary directory to a flat structure without the directories. You can use a command like `unzip -j adf_essentials.zip` to achieve this.

> A default unzip will unpack to the same directory structure as the ZIP file. This will not work. You must unpack everything into one directory, ignoring the directory paths in the ZIP file.

Copy all the files to the `lib` directory of the GlassFish domain where you want to run ADF Essentials applications. If you performed the installation as described earlier in the chapter, the `lib` directory will be `c:\adfessentials\glassfish3\glassfish\domains\domain1\lib`.

Setting the GlassFish JVM parameters

Because ADF applications are a bit more memory-hungry than the average JEE application, you will need to change the GlassFish JVM settings.

In a web browser, go to the GlassFish Administration page (by default on port 4848 of the server where you installed GlassFish, for example, `http://localhost:4848`). Log in with the admin user you created during installation and go to **Configurations | server-config | JVM Settings**. Open the **JVM Options** tab. Find the option **-XX:MaxPermSize=** and set it to **-XX:MaxPermSize=512m** in order to allow GlassFish to allocate more memory than default. Your screen should look like this:

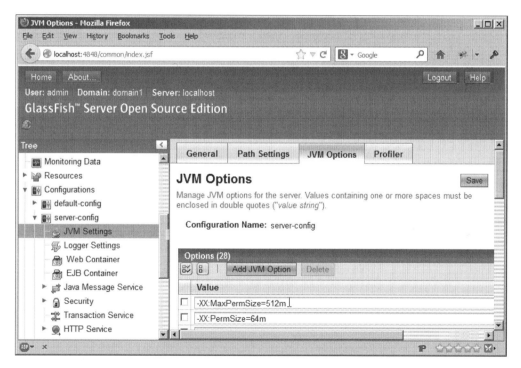

My First ADF Essentials Application

Also, add the new value `-Doracle.mds.cache=simple`.

> This value is read by the ADF framework and instructs it to not use MetaData Services. This feature is not part of ADF Essentials (only of full ADF) — if you forget to set this parameter, your ADF application will fail with an `oracle.adf.share.ADFShareException: getMDSInstance` error.

Then, click on **Save** and restart your GlassFish server. You might notice a **Restart Required** message in the top-left of your server administration window, like this:

You can click on the message to see why a restart is necessary and then click on the **Restart** button, or you can use the commands on the Windows **Start** menu.

Does it work?

There is no easy way to immediately determine if you installed ADF Essentials correctly into your GlassFish server, so we'll get right on to the task of building simple ADF Essentials applications to prove that your ADF Essentials libraries are indeed correctly installed.

Installing JDeveloper

Now your GlassFish server is ready to run ADF applications — but we still need a tool to build them.

JDeveloper or Eclipse?

There are two tools for building Oracle ADF applications: Oracle JDeveloper and Eclipse with Oracle Enterprise Pack for Eclipse. There are two kinds of ADF: Full ADF, which needs a WebLogic server (and a license fee), and ADF Essentials, which is free.

ADF Essentials is enough to build most applications. Some features that are only available in Full ADF include ADF Mobile, ADF Desktop Integration, ADF Security, ADF remote taskflows, MetaData Services, and so on. Refer to the ADF Essentials FAQ for a full list: `http://www.oracle.com/technetwork/developer-tools/adf/overview/adfessentialsfaq-1837249.pdf`.

At the time of writing, JDeveloper was supported for developing both kinds of ADF applications, but Oracle Enterprise Pack for Eclipse is only supported for building applications for Full ADF. We can see the same in the following diagram:

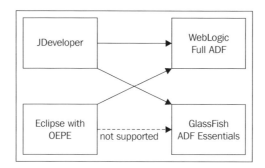

Which JDeveloper?

There are two flavors of JDeveloper:

- The 11g Release 1 branch (called 11gR1, version numbers 11.1.1.x. At the time of writing, the latest was 11.1.1.7.0)
- The 11g Release 2 branch (called 11gR2, version numbers 11.1.2.x. At the time of writing, the latest was 11.1.2.3.0)

11.1.1.7.0 is actually the latest release, and Oracle are developing all of their big internal applications using 11gR1 versions. These are the ones that get bug fixes first and are the only ones to offer support for modern distributed version control tools like Git.

Unfortunately, only the 11gR2 branch has support for GlassFish, so this is the version we have to use for developing applications with ADF Essentials.

 Oracle is promising eventually to bring these two tracks together in a JDeveloper 12c version. If this version is available by the time you read this book, choose that one. It might also have support for GlassFish 4.0.

My First ADF Essentials Application

JDeveloper installation

You can download JDeveloper from the Oracle Technology Network (OTN) website at `http://otn.oracle.com`. Click on the **Downloads** link and you will normally find a link to JDeveloper under **Popular Downloads** to the right. If it's not there, find it via the download index on the left.

Read and accept the OTN JDeveloper License and download the latest version for your platform. At the time of writing, this was 11.1.2.4.0. You'll want the Studio edition because this one includes Oracle ADF. Choose the install for your platform—the Windows install is an `.exe` file, and the Linux install is an executable (`.bin`). For other platforms, you will need to get the Generic installer. If you need the Generic installer, refer to the installation guide (under **Prerequisites & Recommended Install Process**) for detailed instructions. If you're not signed in to `www.oracle.com`, you'll have to do so before you can download.

The installation of JDeveloper on Windows is straightforward—just run the `jdevstudio11124install.exe` file. When prompted for an install directory, select `C:\adfessentials\Middleware111240`. Choose to perform a **Typical** installation.

> If you later decide to install other versions of JDeveloper on your development machine, keep each version in its own directory.

The first time you start JDeveloper, you will be prompted to select a role. Select **Studio Developer** and remove the checkmark in the **Always prompt for role selection on startup** box.

Installing the MySQL Connector in JDeveloper

By default, JDeveloper does not come with a connector to MySQL databases. However, you have already downloaded the JDBC Connector for MySQL (Connector/J) that you can use in JDeveloper as well.

To install it in JDeveloper, copy the `mysql-connector-java-5.1.25-bin.jar` file (or whatever the version number is by the time you read this) to `C:\adfessentials\middleware111240\jdeveloper\jdev\lib`.

> The driver just needs to be placed on JDeveloper's classpath—the preceding directory is one possible option.

Then, from within JDeveloper, choose **Tools | Manage Libraries**. Click on **New** to add a new library and call it **MySQL Driver**. Choose the **Class Path** node and click on Add **Entry**. Navigate to the `C:\adfessentials\middleware111240\jdeveloper\jdev\lib` directory, choose the JAR, file and click on **Select**.

 Choose the JAR file itself, not the directory.

The **Create Library** dialog should look like this:

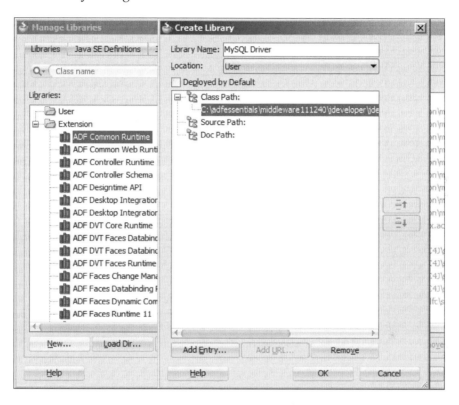

Click on **OK** twice to close the dialog boxes. Now you have the MySQL driver available for your projects.

Installing the GlassFish Server Extension

In order to make it easier to manage the GlassFish server from within JDeveloper, you should install the GlassFish Server Extension into JDeveloper.

My First ADF Essentials Application

In JDeveloper, choose **Help, Check for Updates**. In step 2 of the **Check for Updates** wizard, make sure that **Open Source and Partner Extensions** is checked. In step 3, find the **Glassfish Server Extension** and select it. Click on **Next** and then click on **Finish**, and allow JDeveloper to restart. When JDeveloper starts again, you should see some GlassFish icons on your toolbar, like this:

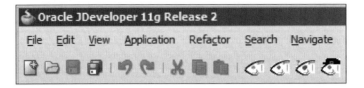

You also need to tell JDeveloper where you have installed GlassFish. Choose **Tools | Preferences | GlassFish Preferences**. If you only see a **Load Extension** button, click on it to load the GlassFish. Then, update all the paths to match your GlassFish installation. If you use the same directories as this book, your dialog box will look like this:

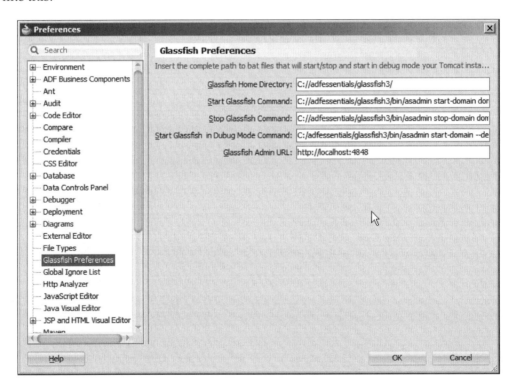

Connecting to the GlassFish server

If your GlassFish server is not running, start it. On Windows, this is done via **Start | GlassFish Server Open Source Edition | Start Application Server**, or you can use the new GlassFish icons on the toolbar in JDeveloper.

Choose **File | New | Connections | Application Server Connection**. Give your connection a name and choose **Glassfish 3.1** as **Connection Type**. In step 2, provide the admin username (admin) and leave the password field blank (the default GlassFish install doesn't set an admin password). In step 3, you can leave the default hostname and ports.

In step 4 of the wizard, test the connection. You should see all tests successful as shown in the following screenshot if your GlassFish server is running and JDeveloper can connect to it:

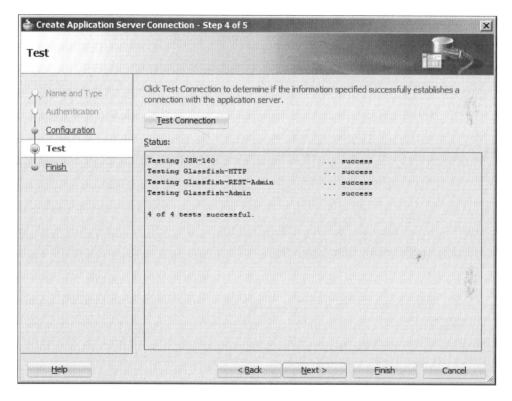

Building a simple ADF Essentials application

All ADF applications consist of the following parts:

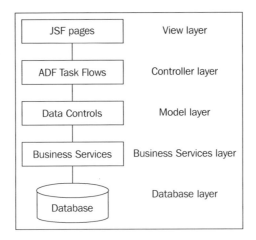

- **View layer**: The View layer consists of your **JSF pages**.
- **Controller layer**: The Controller layer consists of **ADF Task Flows**.
- **Model layer**: The Model layer consists of the **Data Controls** that connect the View/Controller layers to the business service.
- **Business Service layer**: The Business Service layer provides services to query and manipulate data. There are many ways to build business services—in this book, we will use ADF Business Components, but you can also use, for example, JPA Entities and EJB 3.0 Session beans, POJOs, web services, and so on.
- **Database layer**: The Database layer is where your data is stored persistently.

This section will briefly take you through the necessary steps to create an ADF Essentials application with the simplest possible representation of all of these layers. If you follow the steps on your own environment, you will get a first-hand feel for ADF development with JDeveloper. The next chapters will explain the various parts in more detail.

Creating the application

To create the application, click on the **New Application** link in the Application **Navigator** or choose **File** | **New** | **Applications**. Choose **Fusion Web Application** (ADF).

Give your application a name, provide a directory, and enter an application package prefix. This prefix is used in Java package naming in the application, so it should adhere to your normal Java naming standards. If your organization has the Internet domain company.com, your application package prefix will normally be something like com.company.<application>, for example, com.company.adfdemo1.

You can leave the defaults for the **Model** and **ViewController** projects in the following steps of the wizard.

When you are done, your screen will look like the following screenshot, with your application name at the top of the **Application Navigator** to the right, two projects under it, and a quick start checklist for the application in the middle:

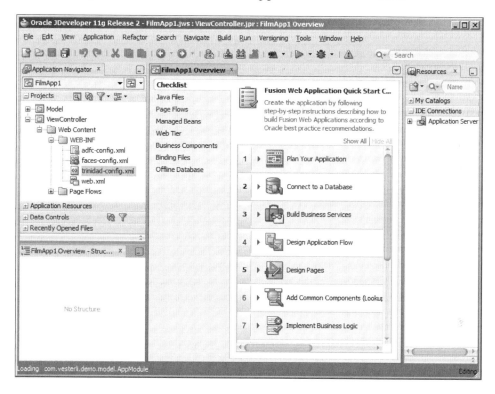

You can explore the checklist to get a feel for the steps in ADF application development—it includes both detailed task lists and links to relevant places in the documentation.

Database

We will be working on the `film` table in the MySQL Sakila demo database. To create a connection, choose **File | New | Connections | Database Connection**. Give your **Connection Name**, choose **Connection Type** as **MySQL**, fill in **Username** as `root`, and give the **Password**. Remember that the default port is 3306 and we use the default `sakila` database. Your screen should look like this:

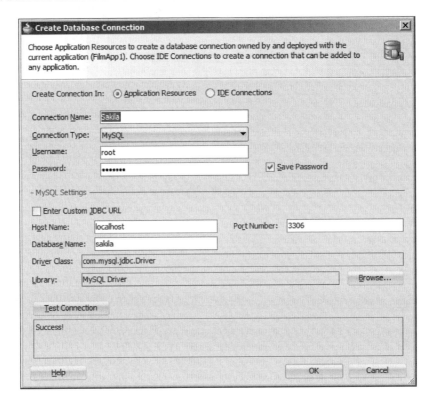

In the **Library** field, click on **Browse** and select the **MySQL Driver** you created when you installed JDeveloper (it's under the **User** node in the **Select Library** dialog).

Click on **Test Connection** – if you get a **Success!** message, your driver is installed correctly and you have provided the right connection information.

Business service

To start building business services for your application, select the **Model** project in the **Application Navigator** and choose **File | New | Business Tier | ADF Business Components | Business Components from Tables** as shown in the following screenshot:

Chapter 1

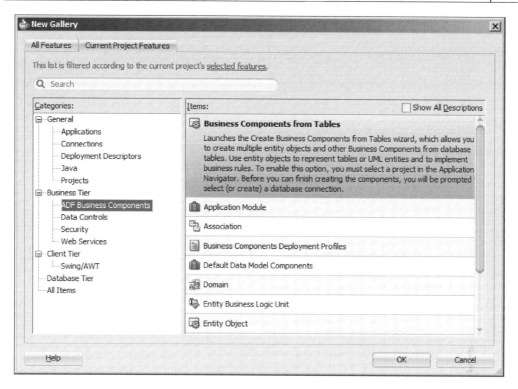

In the **Initialize Business Components Project** wizard, choose your **Sakila** connection, choose **SQL92** as the **SQL Platform**, and choose **Java** as **Data Type Map**.

> The **SQL Platform** setting controls the SQL statements that ADF generates. If you know you'll be using a specific database, you can select it to allow ADF to build optimized SQL for that platform. SQL92 is a standard that is supported by all modern databases, including MySQL.
>
> The **Data Type Map** setting controls the Java objects used by ADF. Unless you are using an Oracle database, select **Java**.

1. In step 1 of the wizard, click on **Query**, choose the `film` table on the left, and use the **>** button to move it to the **Selected** box in order to create an entity object.

2. In step 2, move the `Film` entity object to the **Selected** box on the right in order to create an entity-based view object.

3. In step 3, don't change anything (that is, do not create any query-based view objects).

4. In step 4, leave the defaults (that is, create an Application Module).

[39]

My First ADF Essentials Application

5. In step 5, you can leave the defaults (that is, do not create a business component diagram). If you are curious, feel free to check the checkbox to see the documentation JDeveloper can automatically generate for you.
6. In step 6, just click on **Finish**.

JDeveloper creates a number of objects for you — you can see them in the **Application Navigator**.

You can test your business components by right-clicking on the **AppModule** node (with the suitcase icon) and choosing **Run** as shown in the following screenshot:

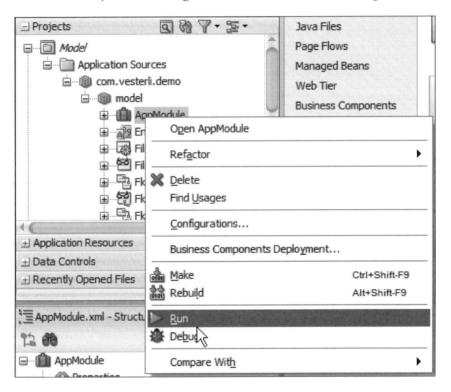

This starts the Business Components Tester application shown in the following screenshot, which allows you to interact with your business service through a simple UI:

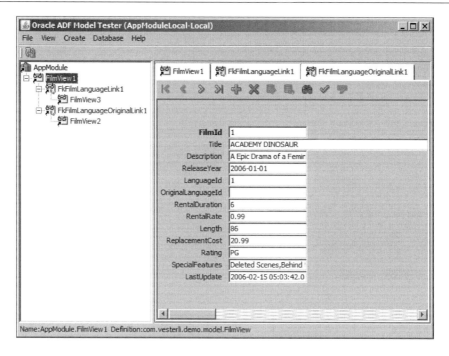

Model layer

The model layer is automatically created for you when you create the business components. You can see the available data elements and operations in the **Data Controls** palette in the **Application Navigator** as shown in the following screenshot:

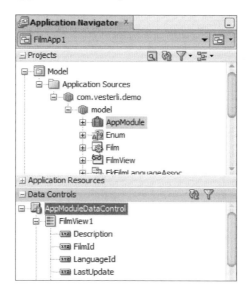

Controller layer

In the controller layer, we define the screens that make up the application and the possible navigation flows between them. For now, we'll just use the **Unbounded Task Flow** that every ADF application has.

Open the **ViewController** project and then **Web Content** | **Page Flows** to see the `adfc-config` element that represents the **Unbounded Task Flow**. Double-click on this element to open a visual representation of the flow. It's empty at the moment because we haven't added any pages yet.

Drag a **View** activity in from the **Component Palette** on the left as shown in the following screenshot and give it a name (for example, `FilmPage`):

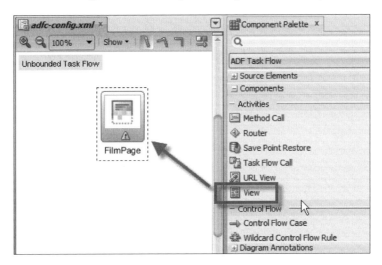

You'll notice that the view component has a yellow exclamation mark, indicating a warning. This means that we have added a view component to the task flow, but we have not actually defined the page yet. So, let's do that.

View layer

In the **View** layer, we define the actual JSF pages that make up the application. Simply double-click on the page you just created in the unbounded task flow to open the **Create JSF Page** wizard. Set **Document Type** to **Facelets** and leave the page layout at **Blank Page**. We'll get back to using layouts and page templates in a later chapter.

Click on **OK** to actually create the page and open it in JDeveloper. You'll see an empty page in the **Design** view.

Find the **Data Controls** panel to the left and expand it. Expand the `AppModuleDataControl` node and drag the `FilmView1` object onto the page as shown in the following screenshot:

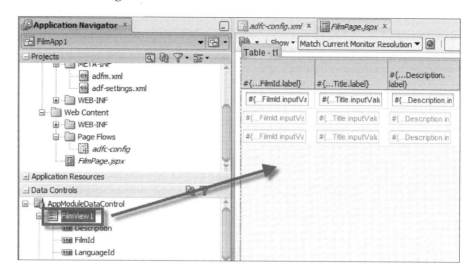

When you release it, JDeveloper will automatically prompt you for a choice of component. Choose **Table | ADF Read-Only Table**. In the **Edit Columns** dialog, check the **Enable Sorting** and **Enable Filtering** checkboxes and click on **OK**.

Your page will show a representation of an ADF table full of mysterious `#{...xxx}` labels and fields. They represent bindings to the data control and will be replaced with actual labels and data at runtime — we'll get back to this in a later chapter.

By default, your application gets a long and complicated URL. You can change this by right-clicking on the **ViewController** project and choosing **Project Properties**. Select the **Java EE Application** node and set the **Java EE Web Context Root** to something simpler. It will typically default to something like `FilmApp1-ViewController-context-root` — you can change this to something like `FilmApp1`.

Click on **Save All** to save your work.

Getting ready to deploy

There are some settings that you need to change in order to make your application run with ADF Essentials on GlassFish.

DataSource

You just want your application to include the name of your database connection, not the actual connection details. In order to ensure this, you need to right-click on your `Model` project and choose **Project Properties**. In the properties dialog, choose **Deployment** and then **Edit** to edit the deployment profile. Choose **Connections** and then **Connection Name Only** as shown in the following screenshot:

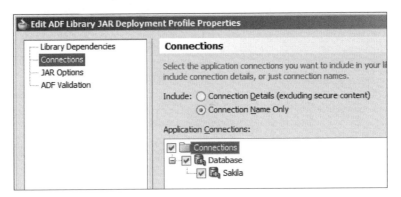

Then, click on **OK** a couple of times to close the dialog box.

Application module configuration

In the current version of JDeveloper, the default application module configuration does not work with GlassFish, so you need to change the `bc4j.xcfg` file.

Right-click on the **Application Module** in the `Model` project and choose **Configurations**. This opens the `bc4j.xcfg` file in the **Overview** mode. Find the **Source** tab at the bottom of this panel to see the actual contents of this file.

Find the two `<Custom JDBCDataSource=.../>` lines. If they start with `java:comp/env`, change them to look like this:

```
<Custom JDBCDataSource="jdbc/SakilaDS">
```

Change platform

Finally, you need to tell JDeveloper that you want to run your ADF Essentials application on the GlassFish platform. You do this in two places:

- In the project properties for the `ViewController` project (choose **Deployment** and edit the deployment profile as shown in the preceding screenshot, choose **Platform**, and then **GlassFish 3.1**) as shown in the following screenshot:

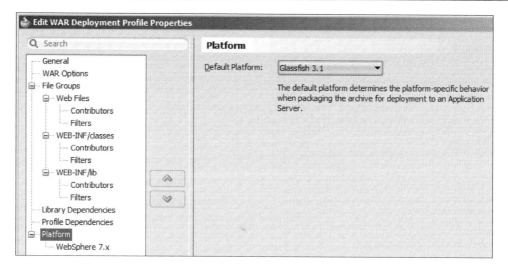

- In the application properties (choose **Application | Application Properties** on the menu, then **Deployment**, and edit the deployment profile as in the preceding screenshot. Choose **Platform** and then **GlassFish 3.1**).

Running your first ADF Essentials application

Now your first ADF Essentials application is ready to deploy and run!

Choose **Application, Deploy**. You should see a default deployment profile (something like `FilmApp1_Project1_FilmApp1`). Choose this default profile and choose **Deploy to Application Server**. Choose your GlassFish connection and click on **Finish** to deploy your application.

The log panel at the bottom of the JDeveloper window will show deployment messages on the **Deployment** tab.

```
[03:34:42 PM] ----  Deployment started.  ----
[03:34:42 PM] Target platform is  (Glassfish 3.1).
[03:34:42 PM] Retrieving existing application information
[03:34:42 PM] Running dependency analysis...
[03:34:42 PM] Building...
[03:34:49 PM] Deploying 2 profiles...
[03:34:51 PM] Wrote Web Application Module to C:\JDeveloper\mywork\FilmApp1\ViewController\deploy\FilmApp1_ViewController_webapp.war
[03:34:55 PM] Wrote Enterprise Application Module to C:\JDeveloper\mywork\FilmApp1\deploy\FilmApp1_Project1_FilmApp1.ear
```

My First ADF Essentials Application

```
[03:34:55 PM] Deploying Application...
[03:38:28 PM] Application Deployed Successfully.
[03:38:28 PM] Elapsed time for deployment:   3 minutes, 46 seconds
[03:38:28 PM] ----   Deployment finished.   ----
```

Have patience—it takes a while (up to several minutes) for JDeveloper to bundle up the necessary ADF Essentials libraries with your application and deploy it onto the GlassFish server.

Once the deployment is finished, you can run your application in a web browser. Your URL will be of the form `http://<server>:<port>/<web context root>/faces/<page name>`. Remember that you set the web context root in the properties of the `ViewController` project. In the preceding section on the controller layer, we set it to `FilmApp1`. An example of a URL would be `http://localhost:8080/FilmApp1/faces/FilmPage.jspx`. Your page should look like this:

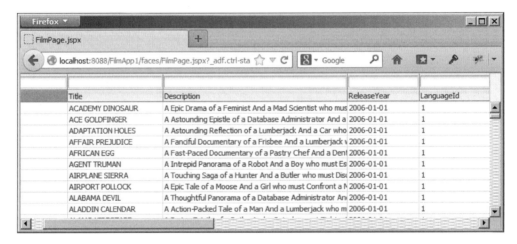

Notice some of the cool features of the ADF table component we used:

- You can resize the columns by dragging the column borders
- You can reorder columns with drag-and-drop
- New records are loaded as you scroll down (try dragging the slider on the vertical scrollbar)
- You can sort columns by clicking on the header
- You can filter data by entering filtering criteria in the filtering field over each column

Can it run faster?

Because the deployment from JDeveloper to GlassFish currently takes quite a long time, many developers choose to run their new code first in the WebLogic server that is pre-integrated into JDeveloper. If you set up WebLogic for MySQL, a simple application like the preceding should be able to start in 20-30 seconds instead of several minutes.

> Hopefully, the deployment speed to GlassFish will be improved in the future. Check out the http://www.adfessentials.com for any tips about speeding up deployment that have been discovered after the publication of this book.

Setting up WebLogic for MySQL

If you want to run MySQL applications in the built-in WebLogic server, you first need to copy the MySQL Connector JAR (mysql-connector-java-5.1.25-bin.jar) to a directory where WebLogic can find it. A good choice is the directory for external libraries in the JRA installation: C:\adfessentials\middleware111240\jdk160_24\lib\ext.

> If you are familiar with WebLogic, you should be able to place the MySQL connector in the WebLogic default domain lib directory. However, in JDeveloper 11.1.2.4, this does not work. Either use the preceding directory or modify the domain startup scripts.

Adding a DataSource to WebLogic

Once you have the driver installed, you need to define a datasource with the right name like you did earlier in the chapter for GlassFish.

First, in JDeveloper, start the built-in WebLogic server with the command **Run | Start Server Instance**. The first time you start the server, you will be prompted for a password to the default domain. Watch the messages in the log window until you see the following command:

    <Server started in RUNNING mode>

Then, open a web browser and type in the address http://localhost:7101/console. Log in with the admin user and the password you provided. After a little while, the WebLogic console window opens.

My First ADF Essentials Application

Expand the **Services** node under **Domain Structure** to the left and select the **Data Sources** node. Click on **New | Generic Data Source**. Give your datasource a **Name** (SakilaDS) and a **JNDI Name** (jdbc/SakilaDS), and choose **Database Type** as **MySQL**. In the next two steps, just leave the defaults. On the **Connection Properties** page, provide your connection details:

- **Database Name**: sakila
- **Host Name**: localhost
- **Port**: 3306
- **Database User Name**: root
- **Password and Confirm Password**: Your database root password, for example, ADFsecret/13

On the following screen, click on **Test Configuration**. You should see **Connection test succeeded**.

Click on **Next** (not **Finish**) and check the checkbox next to **DefaultServer**. Then, click on **Finish**.

> In WebLogic, a JDBC driver definition is by default not connected to any server. If you forget to check the checkbox associating the SakilaDS datasource with the DefaultServer, the server can't connect to the database.

Running your first ADF Essentials application again

To run your first ADF Essentials application in the built-in WebLogic, server simply right-click on FilmPage in the **Application Navigator** and choose **Run**. The application will automatically be re-built, deployed to the built-in WebLogic server, and opened in a browser.

Summary

We've set up the entire infrastructure for building ADF Essentials applications: a MySQL database, the GlassFish server, and the JDeveloper integrated development environment. We have also installed the necessary interconnections and wired everything together so our first ADF Essentials application could run.

In the next chapter, we'll learn more about how to develop business services using ADF Business Components for Java.

2
Creating Business Services

Now that we have set up all the necessary software and have built a simple application to verify it, we can start building real-life ADF applications. Remember that an ADF application consists of the following layers as:

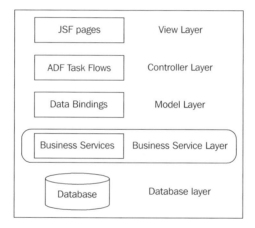

In this chapter, we will concentrate on the **Business Service** layer. First, we will discuss business services in general, then we will build some necessary base components, and finally we will build the necessary **ADF Business Components** (**ADF BC**) for the sample application described in the introduction.

Business service possibilities

The business service layer is doing most of the work that the application performs, such as delivering data, accepting instructions to create, change, or remove data, and performing more complicated calculations and operations. This layer interacts with the user interface part of the application through the use of ADF bindings.

Creating Business Services

There are several ways of building business services in an ADF application, but by far the easiest is to use ADF Business Components (ADF BC) based on database tables. This is the approach taken in this book and in many tutorials on ADF development. If you are just starting out with ADF, you should definitely master this way of building applications first.

Other alternatives are:

- Building **Plain Old Java Objects** (**POJOs**) to encapsulate some other data source (for example, web services) and then creating data controls based on these POJOs.
- Building Business Components on top of other data sources rather than on top of database tables. This approach requires some programming, so it's not recommended until you have some ADF experience.

> If you are just starting out with ADF, build your first applications with ADF BC on database tables. If your architecture requires you to start with ADF and web services in your first ADF application, it is *strongly* recommended that you get someone to help you with the architecture.

The rest of this chapter will discuss ADF Business Components on database tables.

ADF Business Components

The ADF Business Components architecture has five types of components, listed as follows:

- Entity objects
- Entity associations
- View objects
- View links
- Application modules

Chapter 2

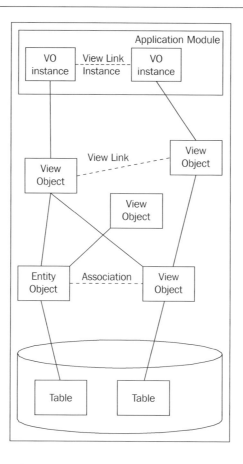

You can think of **Entity Objects** as representations of your database tables – there will be one entity object for every table your application uses.

You can also base Entity Objects on database views, as long as these database views are updatable. See http://dev.mysql.com/doc/refman/5.6/en/view-updatability.html for information on when MySQL views are updatable. In some databases (for example, Oracle), you can define special INSTEAD OF triggers to make views updatable.

Entity objects take care of the object-relational mapping and perform many optimizations for you; for example, entity objects cache data in the middle ties to save database round trips.

Creating Business Services

Similarly, you can think of **Associations** as representations of the relations between tables in your relational database -- there will normally be one association for every foreign key relationship between tables in your database. Interestingly, you can also create associations to represent relationships between tables that are not implemented in the database. So, if your database for some reason does not implement all the foreign keys that are actually part of your business logic, you can add associations in the business service layer.

View Objects represent the datasets you need for a specific purpose -- you can think of them as representations of the SQL SELECT statements you would write to get the data you need. Just like a SELECT statement can join data from multiple tables, a view object can join data from multiple entity objects. Most view objects in your application will be based on data from entity objects. View objects based on a single entity object can be made updatable, while view objects based on several entity objects can typically only update the attributes from one of the view objects. However, if you have a requirement for a very specific dataset and you can write a SELECT statement that retrieves this data, you can create an SQL-based view object. Such SQL-based view objects are of course not updatable.

View objects can have **View Criteria** that represent various filters on the data in the view object. This allows you to define one view object with the data you need and then define multiple view criteria which you can apply in various circumstances.

View Links represent master-detail relationships between view objects. They will typically be based on entity associations (again based on foreign keys in the database), but you can create any view link you like to link two view objects. When view objects are connected with a view link, the ADF framework will automatically handle the master-detail coordination. When you change to another master record, the detail view object will automatically be refreshed with the details for the new master.

Application Modules collect and coordinate a number of view object instances. The application module is the business service that is actually exposed to the user interface as a data control, so in order to use a view object in the user interface of the application, you need to include the view object in an application module. One view object can be used in multiple application modules, and it can even be used in several different roles inside the same application module. The application module handles the database transactions and offers methods to commit or rollback changes to the database across view objects. This gives the developer control over the transactions -- you can allow a user to change data in many view objects without needing to worry about state maintenance; data is not committed until the COMMIT operation is executed.

Starting the example application

Through out this book, we will be building a small application based on the `Sakila` MySQL demo database, which contains data objects for a chain of DVD rental stores.

If you want to follow along in JDeveloper as you read, create a new application using the Fusion Web Application template. Navigate to **File** | **New** to bring up the **New Gallery** dialog box and in this dialog, navigate to **Applications** | **Fusion Web Application (ADF)**.

In step 1 of the wizard, name your application something like `RentalApp` and provide an application package prefix that makes sense to you -- if you work for `company.com`, you could use `com.company.adfdemo`.

> When working through the examples, in this book you can either use the exact example names or modify the names of objects, classes, methods, and so on, slightly from what the book says. If you use the suggested names, you will get through the examples quicker. If you change the names, you will experience some errors as you go along, so it will take longer. However, it will also help you better understand how the different pieces of the ADF puzzle fits together.

Change the default names of the model and view/controller projects to something other than the default (for example, `RentalModel` and `RentalView`). This is a good practice for when you start building larger applications -- you will get confused and there will be naming conflicts in the ADF framework if your application contains multiple projects with generic `Model` and `ViewController` names.

Oracle has published a document called **ADF Naming and Project Layout Guidelines** that you can download from `http://www.oracle.com/technetwork/developer-tools/adf/learnmore/adf-naming-layout-guidelines-v2-00-1904828.pdf`.

How ADF business components work

When you create an ADF business component (entity object, view object, and so on), JDeveloper initially creates only an XML file describing the object (which table, which attributes, and so on). Part of the XML file for an entity might look like as follows:

```
<?xml version="1.0" encoding="windows-1252" ?>
...
<Entity
  xmlns="http://xmlns.oracle.com/bc4j"
  Name="Film"
```

```
      Version="11.1.2.64.36"
      DBObjectType="table"
      DBObjectName="sakila.film"
...
   <Attribute
     Name="FilmId"
     IsNotNull="true"
     ColumnName="film_id"
     SQLType="SMALLINT"
     Type="java.lang.Integer"
     ColumnType="SMALLINT"
     TableName="sakila.film"
     PrimaryKey="true">
...
   </Entity>
```

At runtime, the ADF framework automatically creates and runs the Java classes that read these XML files. For example, ADF creates an instance of the `oracle.jbo.server.EntityImpl` class whenever ADF needs to work with an entity object. The specific instance of the class reads the XML configuration file in order to provide the necessary operations -- for example, if your entity object has a `Title` attribute, the `EntityImpl` class automatically provides a `getTitle()` method.

However, you are not limited to the default behavior of these Oracle-supplied classes. If you want to change the way a business component works, you can. The way you do this is to ask JDeveloper to generate a specific Java class for your business component. For example, if you want your own class for the `Film` entity object, you can open the **Java** tab in the entity object and click on the pencil icon. In the **Select Java Options** dialog, you can click on **Generate Entity Object Class** with some methods, as shown in the following screenshot. In our example, **Accessors** and **Data Manipulation Methods** are selected:

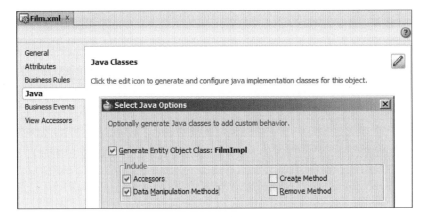

The JDeveloper help explains which methods can be generated.

This creates a Java class that ADF will now use instead of the standard Oracle-supplied `EntityImpl` class. Part of the class is shown as follows:

```
package com.adfessentials.rental.model.entity;
...
public class FilmImpl extends EntityImpl {
...
  /**
   * This is the default constructor (do not remove).
   */
  public FilmImpl() {
  }

  /**
   * Gets the attribute value for Title
   * @return the value of Title
   */
  public String getTitle() {
    return (String)getAttributeInternal(TITLE);
  }

  /**
   * Sets <code>value</code> as the attribute value for Title.
   * @param value value to set the Title
   */
  public void setTitle(String value) {
    setAttributeInternal(TITLE, value);
  }
...
  /**
   * Custom DML update/insert/delete logic here.
   * @param operation the operation type
   * @param e the transaction event
   */
  protected void doDML(int operation, TransactionEvent e) {
    super.doDML(operation, e);
  }
}
```

The class definition shows that your own class (`FilmImpl`) **extends** `EntityImpl`. This is an important concept in Java and other object-oriented languages, and it means that if you don't define anything differently, your own class will work just like the class it extends.

> Immediately after you generate Java, your application works in exactly the same way. The generated code calls methods from the standard Oracle classes to ensure that the functionality does not change. Only when you start modifying the generated code does the application start to behave differently.

Building your own foundation

The ability to create your own Java implementation classes is a powerful feature, but it can be made even more powerful by inserting an extra layer in the object hierarchy.

If you generate Java as described previously, every one of your Java classes is wired directly to one of Oracle's classes. This is not a good idea -- in case you decide that you want some new feature built into every entity implementation class, you would have to change each of the individual classes (`FilmImpl`, `RentalImpl`, and so on).

Fortunately, there is a better way: you can create your own **framework extension classes**. These are sets of classes that extend the Oracle-supplied classes and sit between your specific implementation class and the Oracle-supplied class. For example, you can create your own `com.company.adf.framework.EntityImpl` class that extends the Oracle-supplied class (`oracle.jbo.server.EntityImpl`), and then let your specific implementation classes (for example, `FilmImpl`) extend your own class instead of Oracle's, as shown in the following diagram:

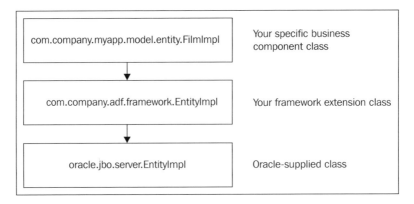

The advantage of this approach is that you have one point under your own control with which to change the general behavior of the entire framework. If you decide to implement, for example, a performance measurement on every UPDATE statement, you can implement this in your own `EntityImpl` class instead of having to wade through and modify every entity object that you have generated Java classes for.

Building framework extension classes

To keep your framework extension classes separate from your application, create a new project for them: navigate to **File | New | Projects | ADF Model Project**. Call your project `FrameworkExtension` and give it a default package that does not contain a specific project. If your company Java package names start with `com.company`, you could choose something like `com.company.adf.framework`.

Inside this project, you need to create four classes:

- `EntityImpl`
- `ViewObjectImpl`
- `ViewRowImpl`
- `ApplicationModuleImpl`

The ADF framework also allows you to extend the other four classes (`EntityCache`, `EntityDefImpl`, `ViewDefImpl`, and `ApplicationModuleDefImpl`), but this is an advanced topic and is very rarely needed.

To create your own `EntityImpl` class, click on your `FrameworkExtension` project and navigate to **File | New | Java | Class**. Give your class the name `EntityImpl` (the package should already be filled in with the project default). Extend `oracle.jbo.server.EntityImpl` and deselect all the checkboxes as shown in the following screenshot:

When you click on **OK**, an empty class opens with content like the following:

```
package com.adfessentials.adf.framework;

public class EntityImpl extends oracle.jbo.server.EntityImpl {
}
```

That's all there is to it! The magic of object-oriented programming comes into play here -- because your class extends the Oracle-supplied class, all of the methods from `oracle.jbo.server.EntityImpl` are available even though you do not write any code. Only in the case where you want to override any of the methods from Oracle's `EntityImpl` class would you add code to your framework extension class.

Similarly, create:

- A `ViewObjectImpl` class extending `oracle.jbo.server.ViewObjectImpl`
- A `ViewRowImpl` class extending `oracle.jbo.server.ViewRowImpl`
- An `ApplicationModuleImpl` class extending `oracle.jbo.server.ApplicationModuleImpl`

For now, we just leave these classes inside the application. In *Chapter 5, Building Enterprise Applications*, you will see how to package your framework extension classes into a reusable **ADF Library**.

Using framework extension classes

Creating the framework extension classes was the first step; the second step is to tell JDeveloper to base all new ADF business components on your classes instead of Oracle's.

To do this, navigate to **Tools | Preferences | ADF Business Components | Base Classes**. Provide the full name (including package) for your own `EntityImpl`, `ViewObjectImpl`, `ViewRowImpl`, and `ApplicationModuleImpl` as shown as follows:

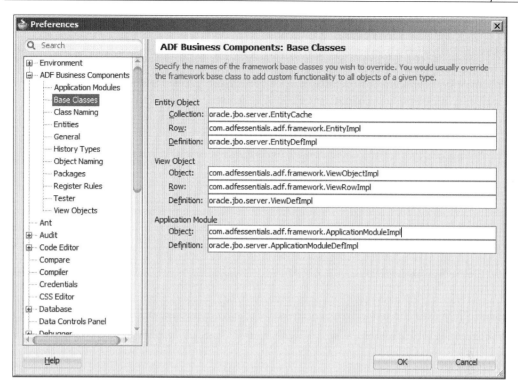

Now you have created your own framework extension classes and have told JDeveloper to always use these from now on. This ensures that you have one central place where you can implement general changes that will apply to every entity object, view object, or application module.

Building entity objects for the example application

In order to illustrate the process of building business components, we will build the necessary objects to show customers and their rentals. This will involve the following objects in the `Sakila` database:

- `customer`
- `rental`
- `inventory`
- `film`

Preparing to build

Before you start creating entity objects, you need to create a connection to the database inside your application. This is done like in *Chapter 1, My First ADF Essentials Application*, by navigating to **File** | **New** | **Connections** | **Database Connection**. Give your connection a name, choose **Connection** type MySQL, fill in username (root), password, port (default is 3306), and database name (sakila). You don't need to select a library again -- JDeveloper has associated the library you defined in *Chapter 1, My First ADF Essentials Application* permanently with MySQL connections.

Another thing you want to do before building the business components is to tell JDeveloper which Java packages the various components go into. Navigate to **Tools** | **Preferences** and then **ADF Business Components** | **Packages**. Fill in this dialog as shown in the following screenshot:

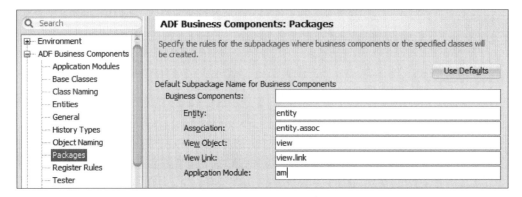

These settings will place the five different types of business components in different Java packages for a better overview in the **Application Navigator** in JDeveloper.

Finally, you need to tell JDeveloper that your **RentalModel** project has a dependency on the **FrameworkExtension** project. This is necessary because you have configured JDeveloper to base all new business components on your own framework extension classes. In a real-life enterprise application, you would use an ADF Library for this purpose; we'll return to this topic in *Chapter 5, Building Enterprise Applications*.

Right-click on your model project and choose **Project Properties**. Then choose the **Dependencies** node and click on the little pencil icon on the right. Open the FrameworkExtension node and check the **Build Output** checkbox as shown in the following screenshot:

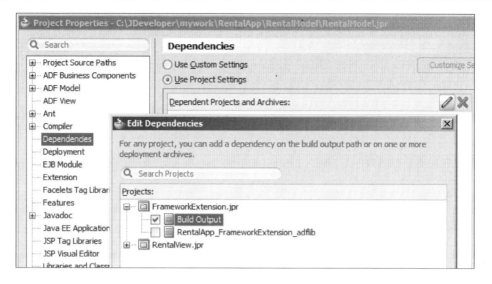

Then click on **OK** a couple of times to close all the dialogs.

Also define a similar dependency on FrameworkExtension in your **View** project.

Running the wizard

Click on the model project (**RentalModel** or similar) and start the **Business Components from Tables** wizard (**File | New | Business Tier | ADF Business Components | Business Components from Tables**). Remember to choose **SQL92** as the **SQL Platform** and choose **Java** as **Data Type Map**.

>
> The **SQL Platform** setting controls the SQL statements that ADF generates. If you know you'll be using a specific database, you can select it to allow ADF to build optimized SQL for that platform. **SQL92** is a standard that is supported by all modern databases, including MySQL.
>
> The **Data Type Map** setting controls the Java objects used by ADF. Unless you are using an Oracle database, click on **Java**.

In step 1 of the wizard, click on **Query**, choose the customer, film, inventory, and rental tables on the left, and use the **>** button to shuttle them to the **Selected** box. Then simply click on **Finish** to create the entity objects (we'll create the other business components outside of this wizard).

Creating Business Services

The **Application Navigator** will show the many objects JDeveloper has created for you:

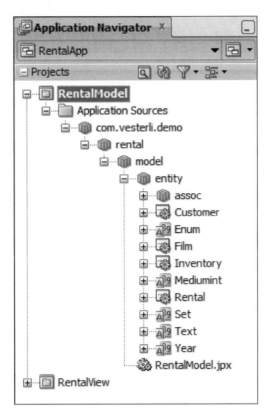

In addition to the entity objects in the `.entity` package, there are also a lot of associations in the `.entity.assoc` package.

Examining the result

You can see that there are two types of objects here: the actual entity objects (the icons with a little gearwheel) and some **Domains** (with a letter and digits icon):

- An ADF domain is a special data type that JDeveloper creates whenever it is not able to map a database column directly to a Java type.

- The Enum domain is created for the enumeration column rating in the table film. This enumeration limits the values in this column to the normal US film ratings: G, PG, PG-13, R, and NC-17. Because such a Java object does not exist, a domain is created.
- The Mediumint domain is created for the inventory_id column from the rental table, which is of the MySQL data type MEDIUMINT.
- The Set domain is created for the special_features column in the film table. This column is of the special MySQL SET type (a kind of collection of binary flags where each bit corresponds to a specific text, allowing the column to have multiple values).
- The Text domain is created for the description column in the film table. It's simply a longer text than a VARCHAR.
- The Year domain is created for the release_year column in the film table. This column is of the MySQL data type YEAR.

Setting the labels

In the entity objects, you can define the default labels for the user interface. To do this, choose the **Attributes** subtab, select an attribute, and choose the **UI Hints** tab below the attribute list. Here, you can set the **Label** attribute. If you don't override it later, this label will be used in the user interface.

You can also set **UI Hints** in the view objects -- these override any hints defined in the entity objects.

Autogenerated values

In the Sakila database, the _id columns (customer_id, rental_id, and so on) are defined as AUTO_INCREMENT. This means that the database will automatically provide a value when you create a new record.

By default, ADF recognizes that the _id columns are mandatory in the database, but does not recognize that a value will be automatically provided. To prevent errors in your application, you therefore have to uncheck the **Mandatory** checkbox for all key attributes. Open each entity object, click on the key attribute (marked with a little key icon), and uncheck the **Mandatory** checkbox.

Creating Business Services

Your screen should look as shown in the following screenshot:

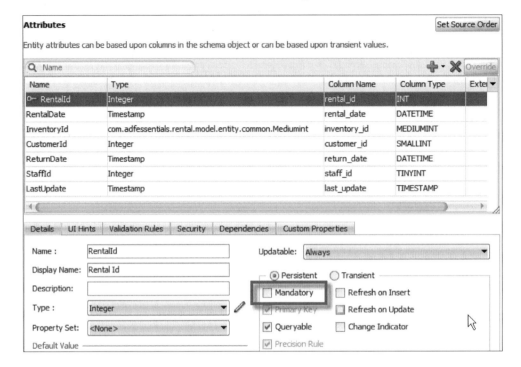

 There is a **Refresh on Insert** setting that instructs ADF to automatically query the new ID value back from the database. Unfortunately, this currently only works on Oracle databases because ADF uses special Oracle SQL syntax (the `RETURNING` keyword) to immediately get the newly created primary key value back from the database.

Cleaning up the data types

Working with custom domains is more complicated than working with standard Java data types, so in the interest of simplicity, we will remove some attributes and change others to standard data types.

First, double-click on the **rental** entity object to open it. Choose the **Attributes** tab on the left, right-click on the **InventoryId** column, and click on **Change Type** as shown in the following screenshot:

[64]

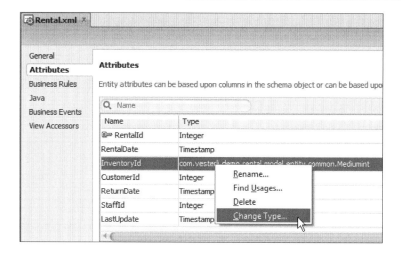

Select the **Integer** type.

> A TINYINT, SMALLINT, MEDIUMINT, and INTEGER can always be converted into a Java Integer. A BIGINT has to be converted to a Java Long.

Then open the `film` entity object and make the following changes:

- Change the type for the `Description` attribute to `String`
- Change the type for the `ReleaseYear` attribute to `Integer`
- Change the type for the `Rating` attribute to `String`
- Delete the `SpecialFeatures` column

We're bypassing the complexities of handling MySQL SET columns by simply deleting the column. If you have to work with an existing database with SET columns and you can't change that, be prepared for some complex coding.

We're also taking a shortcut by simply representing the rating ENUM as a String – this means that our business service doesn't know about the restriction on the data imposed on the database, as it should.

> You can find instructions on how to represent an ENUM as an ADF domain on Duncan Mill's blog at https://blogs.oracle.com/groundside/entry/mysql_adf_business_components_enum.

Navigate to **File** | **Save All** to save your changes.

Creating Business Services

Cleaning up the associations

In the current version of JDeveloper, the **Business Components from Tables** wizard doesn't really understand MySQL databases very well and generates way too many associations, as shown in the following screenshot:

If you look at the database model as shown in the following diagram, you will see that there are actually only three foreign key relationships in the database between these tables:

Chapter 2

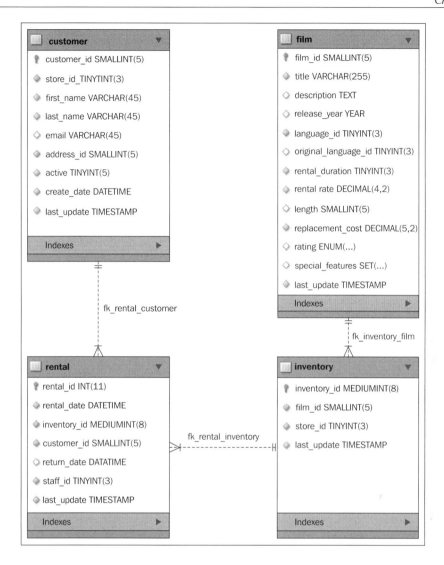

Deleting superfluous associations

If your model shows this problem, first delete all the superfluous associations:

- Delete all `FkCustomerAddress*` associations (4).
- Delete all `FkCustomerStore*` associations (4).
- Delete all `FkFilmLanguage*` associations (8).
- Delete all `FkFilmLanguage*` associations (4).

Creating Business Services

- Delete `FkInventoryFilmAssoc1`, `FkInventoryFilmAssoc2`, and `FkInventoryFilmAssoc3` (3). Leave `FkInventoryFilmAssoc`.
- Delete all `FkInventoryStory*` associations (4).
- Delete `FkRentalCustomerAssoc1`, `FkRentalCustomerAssoc2`, and `FkRentalCustomerAssoc3` (3). Leave `FkRentalCustomerAssoc`.
- Delete `FkRentalInventoryAssoc1`, `FkRentalInventoryAssoc2`, and `FkRentalInventoryAssoc3` (3). Leave `FkRentalInventoryAssoc`.
- Delete all `FkRentalStaff*` associations (4).

You should now only have the three associations that match the actual data model. The application navigator should look as follows:

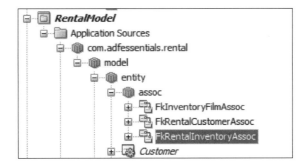

Fixing wrong associations

Next, you may need to fix the association attributes. Open the **FkInventoryFilmAssoc** association, choose the **Relationship** subtab, and click on the pencil icon next to **Attributes** as shown in the following screenshot:

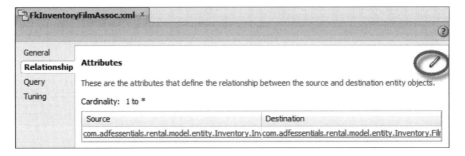

In the **Edit Attributes** dialog, check the existing mapping. It should show **Cardinality** as **0..1 to ***, **Source Attribute** should be **Film.FilmId**, and **Destination Attribute** should be **Inventory.FilmId**. See the following screenshot:

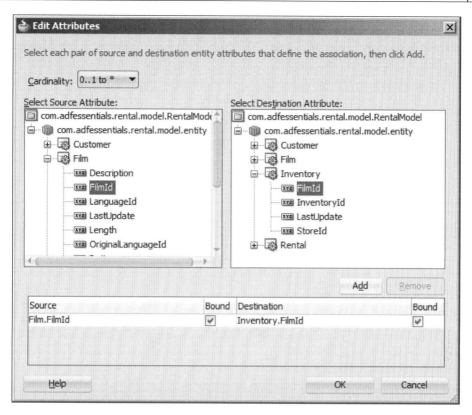

This means that each **Film** item may be referenced in one or more **Inventory** records. Each **Inventory** item represents a specific, physical DVD, whereas the **Film** item represents the film itself.

It may instead show something like `Inventory.InventoryId` mapped to `Inventory.FilmId`. If your association does not look like the preceding screenshot, select the mapping in the lower part of the dialog box and click on **Remove**, and then select the correct mapping in the top part of the dialog box and click on **Add**.

Similarly, ensure that:

- `FkRentalCustomerAssoc` maps `Customer.CustomerId` to `Rental.CustomerId`
- `FkRentalInventoryAssoc` maps `Inventory.InventoryId` to `Rental.InventoryId`

All three associations should have **Cardinality 0..1 to ***.

Navigate to **File** | **Save All** to save your changes.

Creating Business Services

Removing invalid references from entity objects

When you remove associations, JDeveloper sometimes does not clean up the entity objects correctly. Open all your entity objects (`Customer`, `Film`, `Inventory`, and `Rental`) and change to the **Source** view.

If there are orange markings in the right-hand margin of an entity object source window as shown in the following screenshot, it indicates a warning:

If you see any of these warnings, click on each orange bar to jump to the offending code lines (marked with an orange squiggly underline). Delete any `<AccessorAttribute>` tags that contain orange underlined warnings (from `<AccessorAttribute` until `/>`).

Navigate to **File** | **Save All** to save your changes, when done checking all your entity objects.

Chapter 2

Building view objects

Entity objects are created one-to-one, matching the database tables you will be using -- there are no design decisions to make when creating entity objects. View objects, on the other hand, represent the data you need for a specific use case or screen, so you need to have a good idea of the application you want to build before you can create useful view objects.

The storyboard

For the purpose of this book, we will be building a simple customer lookup screen, followed by a master-detail screen showing customers satisfying the search criteria; and for each customer, the films they have rented and not returned. It should look something like the following diagram:

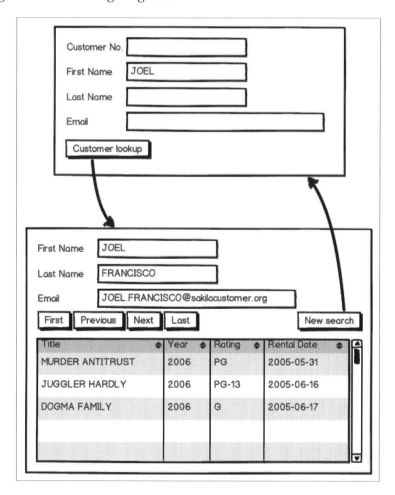

[71]

> Rough sketches of screens like these are called **wireframes**, and a collection of screens with navigation is called a **storyboard**. The preceding diagram was created with the specialized wireframing tool Balsamiq Mockups (http://www.balsamiq.com). It's a good idea for your organization to decide on a common tool to use for creating these first UI sketches.

Looking at this storyboard, we can identify the following data requirements:

- We'll need a customer block showing first name, last name, and e-mail for a customer
- We'll need a rental block showing title, year, rating, and rental date for all the customer's rentals that are not yet returned

Building the customer view object

We'll start with the customer block. This one is easy, because it only needs data from one place: the `customer` table. Click on your model project (`RentalModel` or similar) and navigate to **File | New | Business Tier | ADF Business Components | View Object**:

1. In step 1 of the wizard, give your view object the name `CustomerVO` and leave **Data Source** as **Entity object**.
2. In step 2, open the `.entity` node on the left, click on the `Customer` entity object, and shuttle it to the right-hand **Selected** box.
3. In step 3, shuttle the attributes `FirstName`, `LastName`, and `Email` to the right-hand **Selected** box. You'll notice that the primary key attribute (`CustomerId`) is automatically added as well.
4. In step 4, you don't need to change anything.
5. In step 5, provide an `ORDER BY` clause, for example, `last_name, first_name`.
6. In step 6, you can click on **Finish.** There is nothing to change in the remaining steps of the wizard.

By default, a view object will show records -- in this case, our `CustomerVO` will show all customers. However, we want to be able to limit the data to those that match the search criteria in the first screen. For this purpose, we define a **view criteria** and some bind variables.

You can think of view criteria as predefined filters that you can apply to a view object. A view object can potentially have many different view criteria, allowing you to filter data in various ways. If you do not apply any criteria, you will see the unfiltered view object with all records.

Double-click on your `CustomerVO` view object and choose the **Query** tab. Then scroll down and click on the green plus sign next to **View Criteria**. The **Create View Criteria** dialog opens.

You can leave the default criteria name. Click on **Add Item** to add a criteria line, choose the `CustomerId` attribute, and set **Operator** to **Equals**. Change the value for **Operand** to **Bind Variable** and click on the green plus sign to create a new bind variable. The **Bind Variable** dialog appears as shown in the following screenshot:

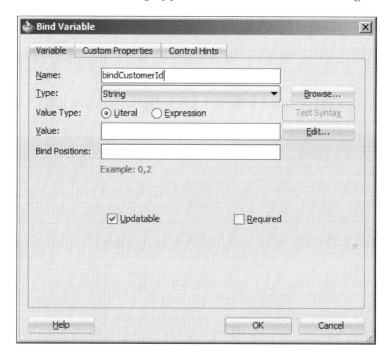

A bind variable is a placeholder for variable data that you need to use in your SQL statement. In this case, we want to be able to compare the `customer_id` in the database to a value passed in to the query through the bind variable.

Creating Business Services

Always use bind variables when you need variable data in your query -- never just use string concatenation to add variables to your SQL. Adding only a string might allow an attacker to place extra SQL statements that you do not want executed. This is called **SQL injection** (see http://en.wikipedia.org/wiki/SQL_injection) and is a very common vulnerability in database applications. Just use bind variables and avoid this.

Give your bind variable a name like `bindCustomerId` and click on **OK** (the rest of the default settings in this dialog are fine). Your dialog should now look as shown in the following screenshot:

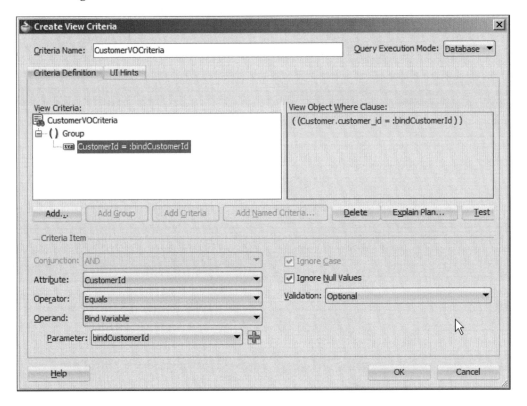

Add another element with the **Conjunction** dropdown set as **OR**, the **Attribute** dropdown set as **FirstName**, the **Operator** dropdown set as **Contains**, and the **Operand** dropdown set as **Bind Variable**. Add a new bind variable called `bindFirstName`.

Similarly, add lines with the **Conjunction** dropdown set as **OR**, for the attributes `LastName` and `Email`, adding new bind variables called `bindLastName` and `bindEmail`.

With all four criteria lines defined, the dialog should look as follows:

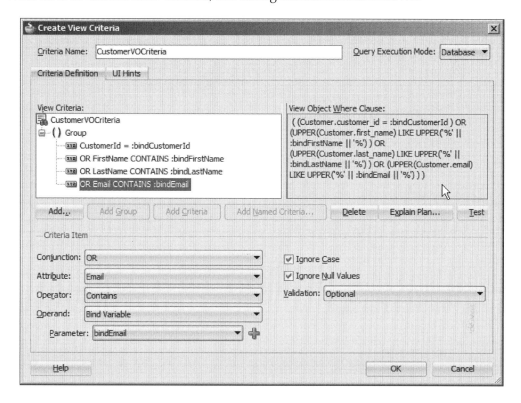

You can see the SQL that will be used at runtime in the right-hand box -- JDeveloper automatically handles null values and case conversion.

Building the rental view object

If you compare the storyboard with the database, you will find that the film title, year, and rating all come from the `film` table, but the rental date comes from the `rental` table. Additionally, you need to go through the `inventory` table in order to connect a `rental` record to a `film` record.

Fortunately, ADF Business Components make it easy to collect data from several entity objects (each corresponding to a specific table) and combine it all in one view object. Select your model project and then navigate to **File** | **New** | **Business Tier** | **ADF Business Components** | **View Object**:

1. In step 1 of the wizard, give your view object the name `RentalVO` and leave **Data Source** as **Entity object**.

Creating Business Services

2. In step 2, open the **.entity** node on the left, click on the **Rental** entity object, and shuttle it to the right-hand **Selected** box as shown in the following screenshot:

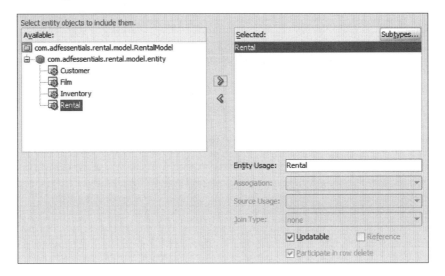

Note that the first view object you select has the **Updatable** checkbox selected by default. If you use several entity objects in a view object, normally only one of them can be updatable.

Then, select the **Inventory** entity object and shuttle it to the right. JDeveloper automatically detects that there is an association between **Rental** and **Inventory** and marks the **Inventory** entity object as a **Reference** object as shown in the following screenshot:

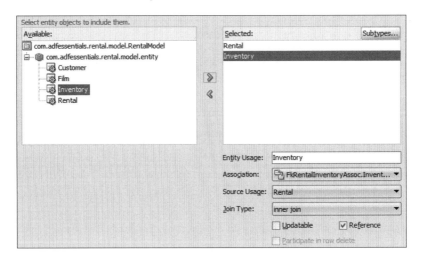

A **Reference** object is normally not updatable -- it just contains additional information that we wish to display to the user. This is useful if your main (updatable) entity object contains key values that point to lookup tables and you want to retrieve the description to display to the user.

Verify the association that JDeveloper has chosen. In this case, the right association is **FkRentalInventoryAssoc.Inventory**.

In a similar manner, select the **Film** entity object and shuttle it to the right, and verify that the association used is **FkInventoryFilmAssoc.Film**.

3. In step 3, shuttle the attributes you need to the **Selected** box on the right-hand side. To be able to create new rental records, include all the entities from the `Rental` entity object (select the **Rental** entity object and click on **>** to include all attributes). Looking at the storyboard, you can see that we additionally need `Title`, `ReleaseYear`, and `Rating` from the `Film` entity object.

   You don't need anything from the `Inventory` entity object -- it's only necessary in order to get from `Film` to `Rental`. You'll notice that the primary key attribute from both `Film` and `Rental` is automatically added as well.

4. In step 4, you don't need to change anything.
5. In step 5, provide an `ORDER BY` clause, for example, `rental_date`.
6. In step 6, you can click on **Finish** -- there is nothing to change in the remaining steps of the wizard.

Now, remember that we only want to show the open rentals: DVDs that have not yet been returned. In order to limit our view object to show only these, we add a query criteria like we did for the `Customer` view object.

> The **Query** tab in the view object (where we add view criteria) also allows us to edit the query itself and add a hardwired `WHERE` clause to the view object. However, such a limitation would always apply, limiting the usefulness of our view object.

Creating Business Services

Double-click on the `RentalVO` view object and create a new view criteria as explained in the preceding section. Call it `UnreturnedCriteria` and add a line saying the `ReturnDate` attribute must be blank. The **Query Criteria** dialog should look like the following screenshot:

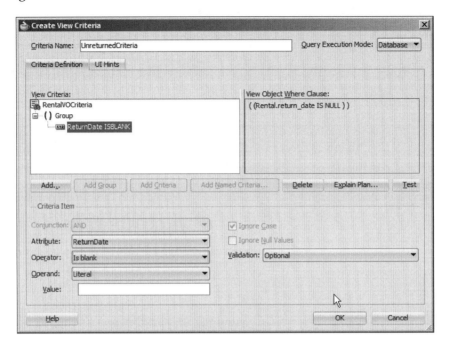

Creating a view link

Now we have the two view objects that contain the necessary data, but we still need to connect them together using a **View Link**. Navigate to **File** | **New** | **Business Tier** | **ADF Business Components** | **View Link** to start the **Create View Link** wizard:

1. In step 1 of the wizard, give the view link a meaningful name (for example, `CustomerRentalLink`).

2. In step 2, leave the **Cardinality** dropdown at **0..1 to ***.

    This means that each source record (customer) may correspond to one or more target records (rentals).

Expand the `CustomerVO` view object node in the left-hand (source) box and select `CustomerId`. Expand the `RentalVO` view object node in the right-hand (destination) box and select the `CustomerId` here as well. Then click on **Add** to add an attribute to the link. Your screen should look as shown in the following screenshot:

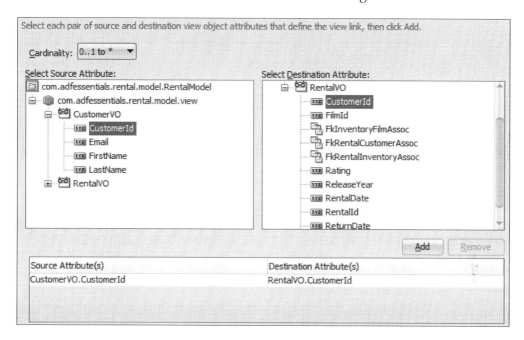

3. In step 3, you can click on **Finish** -- there is nothing to change in the remaining steps of the wizard.

Application module

Now we have two view objects with all the data we need and we have defined the connection between them. The final business component we need to create is an **Application Module**. Navigate to **File** | **New** | **Business Tier** | **ADF Business Components** | **Application Module** to start the **Create Application Module** wizard:

1. In step 1 of the wizard, give the application module a meaningful name (for example, `RentalService`).

Creating Business Services

2. In step 2, expand the **.view** node to see your two view objects. First click on **CustomerVO** on the left. In the **New View Instance** field under the list of available view objects, change the name to `CustomerSearchResult` as shown in the following screenshot:

- Click on the **>** button to create a view object instance in the right-hand box.
- Then expand the **CustomerVO** node to the left to see the node **RentalVO via CustomerRentalLink**. Select this node and give it the name `RentalUnreturned` in the **New View Instance** field, and then shuttle it to the right. It should appear under the **CustomerSearchResult** view object instance in the right-hand side of the dialog.

> Note that there is a difference between selecting **RentalVO via CustomerRentalLink** and just selecting **RentalVO**.
>
> If you base a screen on the **RentalVO** view object without the view link, the screen would always show all rentals across all customers.
>
> If you base a screen on the **RentalVO** view object connected via the view link, it will show only the detail (rental) data that matches the master (customer) record.

- Then click on the **CustomerSearchResult** view object instance and click on the **Edit** button. In the **Edit View Instance** dialog, move the view criteria from the **Available** box to the **Selected** box as shown in the following screenshot:

Chapter 2

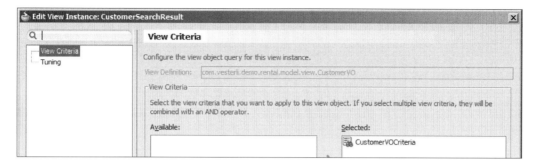

- This applies the view criteria to the specific view object instance in the application module so that when you base a screen on this view object instance, the `CustomerVOCriteria` filter is applied and only the records matching the filter are shown.

 You can have many instances of one view object in the same application module with various combinations of view criteria.

- Similarly, edit the **RentalUnreturned** view object instance and click on **UnreturnedCriteria**.
- Finally, choose the **RentalVO** view object that is *not* connected via the view link, give the view instance the name `RentalVO`, and shuttle it to the right. Your data model window should now look as shown in the following screenshot:

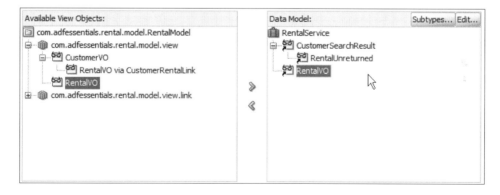

3. In step 3, you can click on **Finish** -- there is nothing to change in the remaining steps of the wizard.

Testing business components

This completes our business service layer. So far, we have created:

- Entity objects
- Associations
- View objects with view criteria
- A view link
- An application module

In many development teams, tasks are split between developers with some building business services and some building the user interface. Naturally, the developers building business services need a way to test their work without having to wait for the UI developers to finish their work. JDeveloper offers this in the form of the Business Components Tester.

To run this tester, simply right-click on the application module and select **Run**. This will start up the built-in tester application that will show the view object instances in your application module, as shown in the following screenshot:

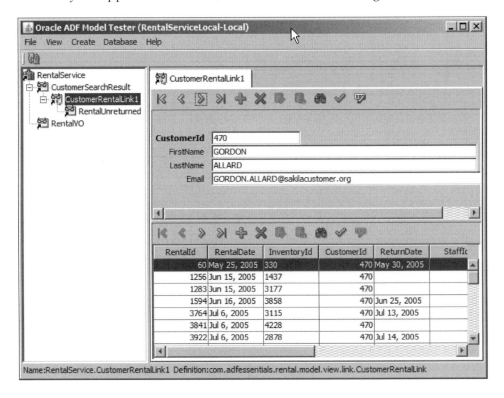

You will be prompted for bind variable values when you activate a view object that needs them.

You can navigate through data, change data, and even create or delete records through the business component tester application.

 If you want to create a rental record, you can leave the `RentalId` column blank, because this value will be provided by the database.

Summary

We have built our own foundation classes for our business components and have created the business services we need for our simple example application. This includes entity objects and associations, view objects, view criteria, a view link, and an application module exposing our business service to the rest of the application. In the next chapter, we will be building the frontend of our application based on these business services.

3
Creating Task Flows and Pages

In *Chapter 2*, *Creating Business Services*, we built the first layer of the application: the **business service** layer. In this chapter, we will build the actual user interface that the user will interact with. This part of the application consists of the **View**, **Controller**, and **Model** layers, as shown in the following diagram:

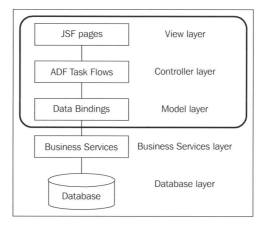

As you may remember from *Chapter 1*, *My First ADF Essentials Application*:

- The **View** layer consists of the pages that are displayed to your users (JSF pages or JSF page fragments)
- The **Controller** layer consists of ADF Task Flows that control the flow between the elements of the view layer
- The **Model** layer consists of the Data Controls that connect the view/controller layers to the underlying business services

Building task flows

A web application consists of a number of pages that must be displayed to the user in a specific sequence. This sequence is not fixed—the user might make a decision as to which page they want to see next, or the application might decide to show a specific page with a warning or a request for more information.

If we did not have a controller layer, each page would have to contain both the actual components on the page as well as the logic to decide where to go next. This intermingling of functionality quickly becomes hard to maintain and is not considered a good programming practice.

That is why we have a controller layer to control the flow through the application. The controller layer manages the logic of what happens in which order so that the individual pages or code elements do not have to worry about this part of the application.

Bounded and unbounded task flows

Every application has one unbounded task flow—we saw that in the simple demo application in *Chapter 1, My First ADF Essentials Application*. In addition, an application may have any number of bounded task flows.

The unbounded task flow is the outer shell of the application, and every page you include in this task flow can be accessed directly through its own URL. If you intend for your application to have multiple entry points, you need to create one page for each entry point.

Most applications, however, mainly make use of bounded task flows. As the name implies, they have the benefit of a well-defined boundary: there is exactly one entry point where a bounded task flow starts when it is called. It can have one or more exit points, potentially returning a value to the calling task flow to allow the caller to make a decision based on what happened in the called task flow. A task flow is designed visually and might look like this:

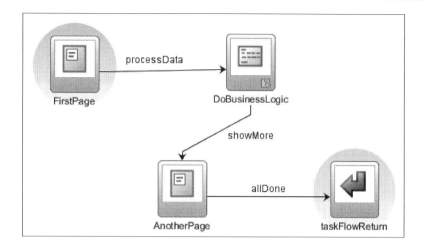

Pages and fragments

Your bounded task flows can contain either **pages** or **page fragments**.

As the name implies, a page is complete and takes up the entire browser window. An application with pages feels like a classic website. Whenever you click on a button or link on the page, the whole screen is redrawn, showing a new page.

A page fragment, on the other hand, is intended to take up only part of a page. This means that a bounded task flow using fragments must live within the context of a page, as shown in the following diagram:

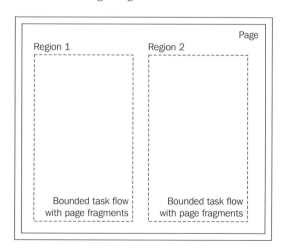

As the diagram shows, a page can contain several regions, each displaying one bounded task flow with page fragments.

Creating Task Flows and Pages

This allows you to build a web application that feels more like a desktop application. If the user clicks on a button or a link in the region to the left, the bounded task flow might advance to another page fragment. However, only the left-hand side of the page is redrawn—the page itself is not reloaded, and the region on the right is also untouched.

 The technical term for this behavior is called **partial page rendering**—only the part of the page that needs to be refreshed is actually changed.

Task flow templates

We saw in *Chapter 2, Creating Business Services* that it was a good idea to build framework extension classes and base our application on these. Even if we don't yet know what we want to place in these classes, it takes only a little time at the beginning to avoid much wasted time later in the project.

Similar to the framework extension classes, we build task flow templates before we start building actual task flows. You can leave them blank for now; they are simply placeholders that we create just in case.

To build a task flow template, select your RentalView project and choose **File | New, JSF/Facelets, ADF Task Flow Template**. Give your template a name like `rental-task-flow-template` and make sure **Create with Page Fragments** is checked as shown in the following screenshot:

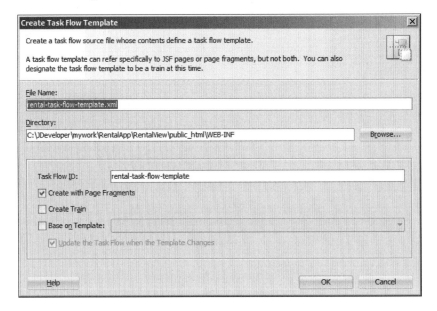

Notice the **Base on Template** checkbox and selection. In ADF 11gR2, you can create a hierarchy of task flow templates. Keep this in mind when you start building large enterprise applications.

When you click on **OK**, the task flow template opens in the work area in JDeveloper with the text **Drop content onto this blank diagram...** in the center. Since we won't be putting any content into our task flow template at this time, you can simply close this diagram.

Example application

In order to demonstrate the use of task flows, we will expand our simple rental application a little. In *Chapter 2, Creating Business Services,* you saw a storyboard showing two screens for finding a customer and his or her pending rentals. In addition to this, we will create another task flow that just contains one page — this one is for registering a new rental.

Building the Rent DVD task flow

We'll start with the very simple Rent DVD task flow. Choose **File** | **New** | **JSF/Facelets** | **ADF Task Flow**. Give your task flow a name like `rent-dvd-flow` and check the **Base on Template** checkbox. When you select this checkbox, the drop-down list becomes active. Because we have only one task flow template in the application and we have not imported any libraries, the select list contains only one template. Leave the checkbox **Update the Task Flow when the Template Changes** checked to make the task flow reference the template (so that any later changes to the template will take effect in the task flow).

> If you don't check the **Update...** checkbox, the template is simply copied into the project and any later changes to the template will not affect the task flow.

When you click on **OK**, the empty task flow opens as shown in the following screenshot:

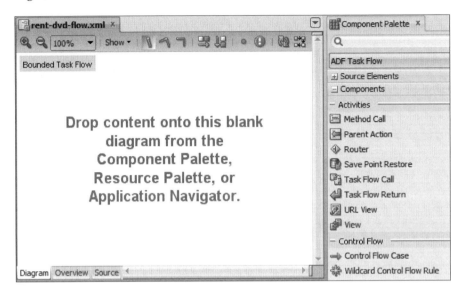

Notice the tabs **Diagram**, **Overview**, and **Source** at the bottom of the window. These allow you to view the task flow in various ways:

- The **Diagram** view allows you to edit your task flow visually by dragging components in from the Component Palette to the left
- The **Overview** view allows you to change various other settings for the task flow through dialog boxes and select lists
- The **Source** view shows the raw XML file that JDeveloper is actually storing

It doesn't matter which view you use to make a change—these views are just different representations of the same task flow definition file.

In this simple case, we'll just drag a view object onto the task flow from the **Component Palette**. Give it a name like rentDvd as shown in the following screenshot:

Chapter 3

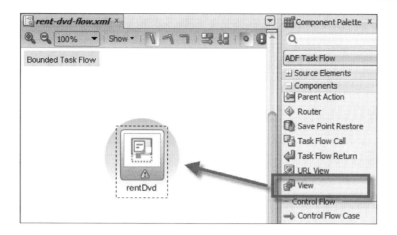

Notice two things about this view:

- The yellow warning icon indicates that there is something wrong with this view—in this case, there is no actual page fragment behind the view yet. So far, we have only told JDeveloper that we have an intention to create a page fragment—we'll put content into it later in this chapter. Also, note that JDeveloper tries to show you that the view is not yet complete by showing the lower half of the symbol with a dashed line—a completed view looks like this:

- The view has a green halo behind it. This indicates that this element is the first one in the flow—this is called the **default activity**. You can have many different components in a task flow, but only one can be the default activity. This is central to the concept of a bounded task flow: it has one well-defined entry point. To change this, right-click on an activity and choose the **Mark Activity** or **Unmark Activity** menus.

 All elements can be the default activity—not just views.

Building the Return DVD task flow

You probably remember from the storyboard in *Chapter 2, Creating Business Services* that the Return DVD storyboard showed two pages, so our task flow will contain two views representing these.

Create a new task flow called something like `return-dvd-flow` with the same settings as the previous task flow. When the empty task flow opens, drag two views onto the canvas, giving them the names `findCustomer` and `showRentals`. Make sure `findCustomer` is the default activity (with the green halo) as shown as follows:

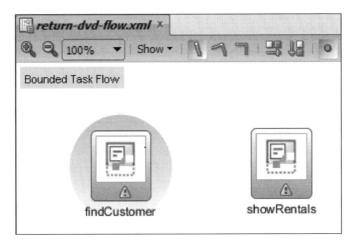

It is easy to determine which views you need in a task flow, because these are explicitly part of your storyboard. It takes a bit of ADF knowledge to figure out what other elements you might need. In this case, we use the first view (`findCustomer`) to gather query values for the customer, and the second view (`showRentals`) to show the result. In between, we need to actually execute a database query using the values from the first screen. Fortunately, JDeveloper makes it really easy to include code in a task flow in the form of method call activities.

When we created our business components in *Chapter 2, Creating Business Services*, the ADF framework automatically provided us with a long list of standard operations that you can see in the **Data Controls** panel in the **Application Navigator** as shown in the following screenshot:

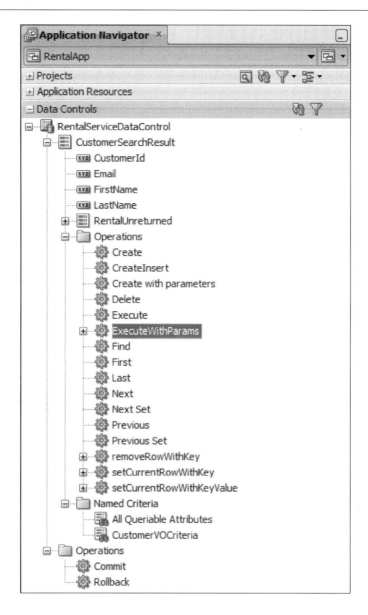

Notice that some of these operations belong to the view object instances in the application module (**Create**, **CreateInsert**, **Create with parameters**, and so on) and some belong to the application module itself (**Commit** and **Rollback**, at the bottom). The operations are marked with little gearwheel icons to show that they are operations, not data. Operations can be dragged directly onto task flows—when you drop them, JDeveloper will automatically create a corresponding method call activity.

Creating Task Flows and Pages

In this case, we need an operation that executes the view object, applying any query criteria. This operation is called **ExecuteWithParams**, and it executes the necessary SQL to fill the view object with all the records that match the parameters.

> The built-in view operations are documented in the Oracle Fusion Middleware Fusion Developer's Guide for Oracle Application Development Framework manual. To find the right place, you can place the cursor on a view object instance in the **Data Controls** palette and press *F1* to call up, JDeveloper help. You should see the help topic **Application Navigator – Data Controls Panel**, and at the bottom of this is a link to the relevant place in the Fusion Developer's Guide.

Find the **ExecuteWithParams** operation and drop it between the two views. An **Edit Action Binding** dialog pops up prompting you to enter values for the bind variables used in the view criteria as shown in the following screenshot:

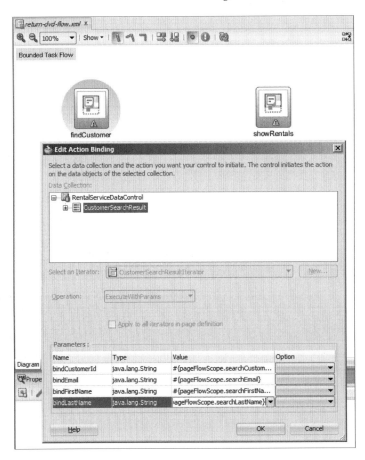

Fill in the **Parameters** section of this dialog as follows:

Name	Value
bindCustomerId	#{pageFlowScope.searchCustomerId}
bindEmail	#{pageFlowScope.searchEmail}
bindFirstName	#{pageFlowScope.searchFirstName}
bindLastName	#{pageFlowScope.searchLastName}

Be very careful to make sure that you write the values exactly like this. The hash sign and the curly brackets identify the value as an Expression Language expression, so they must be written exactly.

The text pageFlowScope (notice the use of uppercase F and S) defines a memory scope—in this case, we are referring to variables that are available throughout the life of the task flow.

> **Memory scopes**
>
> When you use variables and managed beans (more on these in *Chapter 4, Adding Business Logic*), you define their scope. In this case, we use PageFlow scope—refer to the following section on *Memory scopes* for more information.

The last part (searchLastName, and so on) is the only part that you can choose freely. This is just the name of a variable—Expression Language does not require you to define variables, so you can use any name you like. However, you must of course remember the variable names (or write them down) because we have to assign values to them when we start building the pages.

When you click on **OK**, you will see an ExecuteWithParams method call activity added to your task flow.

Creating Task Flows and Pages

The last thing you need to do is to define the navigation between the elements in your task flow. This is done with control flow cases. You find these in the **Component Palette**—obviously, these are the arrow symbols:

1. In your Return DVD task flow, click on **Control Flow Case** in the **Component Palette**, click on the `findCustomer` view, then move the mouse cursor to the `ExecuteWithParams` operation and click on it. These two elements are now connected, and you can provide a name for the control flow. Call this one something like `executeQuery`.
2. Connect the `ExecuteWithParams` operation with the `showRentals` view in a similar way and call this connection something like `showResult`.
3. Select the `ExecuteWithParams` operation, and in the **Property Palette**, set the value of the **Fixed Outcome** property to `showResult`.
4. Connect `showRentals` back to `findCustomer` with a connection called `newSearch`.

Your task flow should now look something like this:

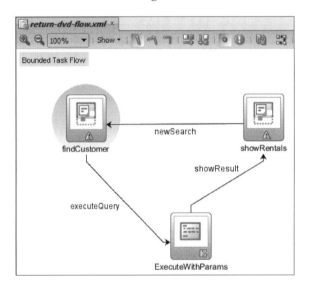

If you did not change the **Fixed Outcome** property of the `ExecuteWithParams` operation, you will see a warning icon next to your control flow case. This is because its name doesn't match with the outcome from the element it's pointing away from. The default outcome of the `ExecuteWithParams` operation is called `ExecuteWithParams`, so if you change the control flow case to something else (like we did previously), you also need to change the **Fixed Outcome** property to match. The drop-down value for this property will only show the control flows leading away from the operation.

That is all we need to do right now to define the controller layer of our simple DVD rental application.

Memory scopes

Variables and managed beans have a scope that determines for how long a variable or a bean lives. It is good practice to use as short a scope as possible—this allows ADF to free up memory as soon as possible and avoids mysterious bugs caused by old values that are not refreshed.

Because ADF is based on **JavaServer Faces (JSF)**, the five standard scopes of JSF are available. In addition, ADF adds three new scopes. When starting out with ADF development, you can get by with the following scopes:

- **The BackingBean scope**: This is a short scope; objects in this scope only live for one request from the client to the server. Use this scope for backing beans (described in *Chapter 4, Adding Business Logic*) that just need to perform an operation and do not need to store data.

> If you know JSF, you might be familiar with the Request scope. In an ADF application where several fragments can coexist on a page, you should use the BackingBean scope where you use the Request scope in a plain JSF application.

- **The PageFlow scope**: This is an intermediate scope; objects in this scope live for the duration of a bounded task flow, across individual pages. Use this scope for beans and variables that need to store data used on several pages in a page flow.
- **The Session scope**: This is a long scope; objects in this scope live for as long as the user has a session with the server (typically until the session times out or the user closes the browser). This scope is shared across all instances of the application.

> Be careful with the Session scope! If your user opens the application multiple times in separate browser tabs, objects in the Session scope might be shared across tabs (depending on browser make, version, and settings). A user will typically consider the application instances in the tabs to be separate, so will consider it a bug if the search result in one tab suddenly shows up in another tab.

Variables and beans should have the shortest scope that still fulfills the application requirements. If you are in doubt, PageFlow scope is often a good choice. As you become more proficient with ADF, you'll want to read the description of memory scopes in section 5.6 in the Oracle Fusion Middleware Web User Interface Developer's Guide for Oracle Application Development Framework. At the time of writing, this document (for JDeveloper 11.1.2.4) could be found at `http://docs.oracle.com/cd/E37975_01/web.111240/e16181/af_lifecycle.htm#CHDGGGBI`.

Other elements of task flows

In addition to the elements we have used previously, you will find some other components in the **Component Palette** for a task flow. The most commonly used are:

- **Router**: The router components are, used to make decisions in the flow. You create a number of control flows leading away from the router, and based on the expressions you define, the router will select one of these. A router always has a default outcome and can have any number of additional cases, each with its own expression. You must define control flows matching all the possible outcomes of the router component.

> Make sure your cases do not overlap, for example, do not have both greater than 5 and greater than 10; you will get weird results.

- **Task flow call**: The task flow call components are used to call a bounded task flow. You normally don't use this from the **Component Palette, but rather** you drag a task flow onto the canvas and JDeveloper creates a task flow call for you. Similar to a router component, a task flow call can have multiple outcomes, and ADF will pick the navigation case that matches the outcome.

- **Task Flow Return**: The task flow return components are used to indicate the end of processing in a bounded task flow and to define the outcome.

The task flow call and task flow return components work together to let a calling task flow take decisions based on what happened in a called task flow. For example, your `new-rental-flow` might call a `customer-create-flow`. The `customer-create-flow` could have two different task flow returns based on whether a new customer was created or not. These could have the outcomes `CustomerCreated` and `CustomerCreateCancel`, and the calling task flow could use a router component after the task flow call to handle the two different cases by showing different pages to the user.

Building pages

With the task flows defined, we are done with the controller layer in our model-view-controller architecture. The next layer we will work on is the view layer.

Using templates

Just like you created a task flow template before you built the first task flow, you should create templates for your pages and page fragments. Page and page fragment templates are always referenced (never copied), so any change you make to a page template will affect all pages based on the template. For now, we will build the templates in the `RentalView` project—in *Chapter 5, Building Enterprise Applications*, we'll see how templates can be kept in their own library in an enterprise application.

Your application will have both a page template and a page fragment template as shown in the following diagram:

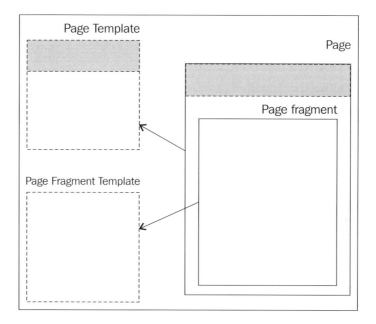

The page is based on the page template and contains task flows with page fragments. Each fragment is based on a separate page fragment template.

Facet definitions

In JSF terminology, a facet is a place where you can place your components. A page can have multiple facets for different parts of the page. When you create a page template, you first define the facet names and then place a `FacetRef` component in the place in your layout where you want the template user to be able to place content.

Page fragment template

Your page fragment template will typically be empty or almost empty, because page fragments are used inside pages. This means that the common visual elements like headers, logos, and so on, should not be part of your page fragment template. We are creating a page fragment template in order to have a place to put common elements in case we later find out that we need them.

To create it, select the **RentalView** project and choose **File | New | Web Tier | JSF/Facelets** and then **ADF Page Template**. The **Create ADF Page Template** dialog opens. Choose **Facelets** as the document type and set the **File Name** to `pageFragmentTemplate.jsf`. The **Page Template Name** should automatically update to match the file name without the extension (`pageFragmentTemplate`).

Because there is no need for your user to access the template directly, you should add `\WEB-INF` to the end of the directory.

 Files placed in the `public_html` directory can be accessed directly, so that is where your pages, images, and stylesheets go. Files placed in `public_html\WEB-INF` are not directly accessible, so that is where your page flow definitions and templates should go.

Choose **Use a Quick Start Layout** and leave the default selection of **One Column** (Stretched). This is the simplest possible layout—we'll see some of the other possibilities when we build the page template.

Use the green plus to define a facet with the name `fragmentContent`. The dialog box should now look like this:

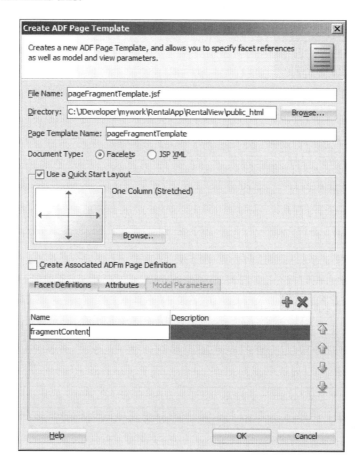

When you click on **OK**, your page template opens in **Design** view. In the **Component Palette**, open the **Layout** node, scroll down to the **Core Structure** heading, and drag a **Facet Definition** onto the center of the page template. You are prompted to select a facet name—since you only defined one, the drop-down list only has one value. Select your content facet and click on **OK**.

In the **Structure** panel (by default placed in the bottom left), you can see the structure of your page template as shown as follows:

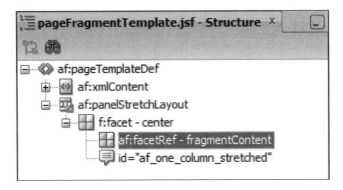

If the **Structure Panel** is not shown, you can choose **View | Structure** to display it. If you can't find it, set **Window | Reset Windows** to **Factory Settings** to display the **Structure Panel** in the bottom left of the JDeveloper window.

You can see that the quick start layout has added an `af:panelStretchLayout` component to the template, and your `af:facetRef` component is placed in the center facet of the `PanelStretchLayout`. Because a `PanelStretchLayout` will stretch whatever is in the center facet to fill the entire available area, this is a good choice for a page fragment template.

Page template

The page template is used for the application pages your user will interact with, so this will contain common visual elements like headers, logos, and so on.

The process to create a page template is very similar to the process of creating a page fragment template. First, select the `RentalView` project and choose **File | New | Web Tier | JSF/Facelets** and then **ADF Page Template**. In the **Create ADF Page Template** dialog, choose `Facelets` as the document type and give your page fragment template a file name like `pageTemplate.jsf`. Again, add `\WEB-INF` to the end of the directory.

Choose **Use a Quick Start Layout** and click on the **Browse** button to see some of the quick start layout options available as shown in the following screenshot:

Chapter 3

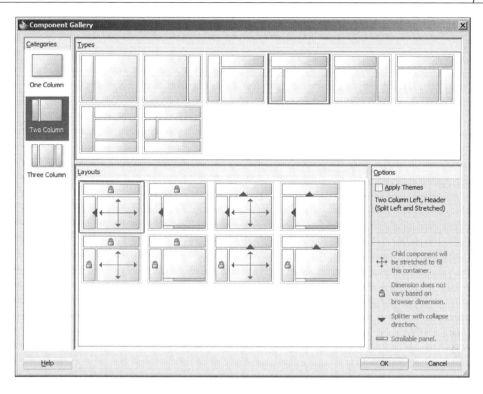

You first choose a category, then a type, and then a layout. Refer to the legend in the bottom-right corner for an explanation of the symbols.

As you learn more about JSF page layout, you will be able to produce these layouts by combining the relevant ADF layout components—the quick start layouts are intended to give you a head start when you first start developing Oracle ADF applications. For the sample application, choose a simple one-column layout, like this:

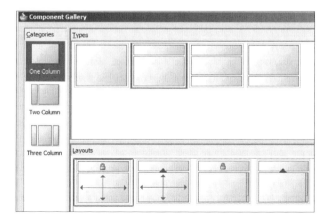

Creating Task Flows and Pages

Like you did for the page fragment template, use the green plus to define a facet, this time with the name `pageContent` as shown in the following screenshot:

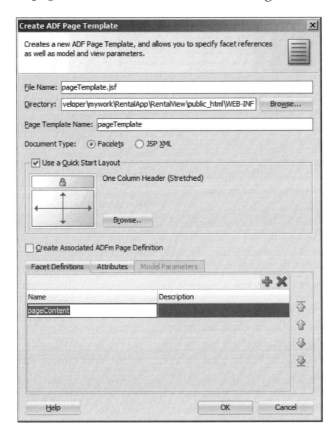

If you choose a more advanced layout, you might want several facets and several corresponding `FacetRef` components, but for the simple application in this book, one facet is enough.

When you click on **OK**, your page template opens in the **Design** view. In the **Component Palette**, open the **Layout** node, scroll down to the **Core Structure** heading, and drag a **Facet Definition** onto the center of the page template. Make sure you drop it on the center of the page canvas (inside the center facet of the `PanelStretchLayout`) and not in the top facet.

 You can also drag components onto the **Structure** panel at the bottom-left—this is just another way of achieving the same goal. In complicated layouts, it can be easier to place components inside the right container by using the **Structure** panel.

Select the facet name when prompted.

To illustrate how to place content on the template, drag an **Output Text** component from the **Component Palette** (found in the **Text** and **Selection** section) and drop it onto the top part of the page template. Use the **Property Inspector** to set the **Value** to `DVD Rental App`.

> **Internationalization**
>
> In this example, we are hard-wiring the text into the template. If there is even the slightest chance that your application will ever need to be translated, you should instead place all your user interface strings in resource bundles. Refer to the Appendix in *Oracle ADF Enterprise Application Development – Made Simple* for more information about internationalization in Oracle ADF.

Next, open the **Style** section to set the color, font size, and font weight as shown in the following screenshot:

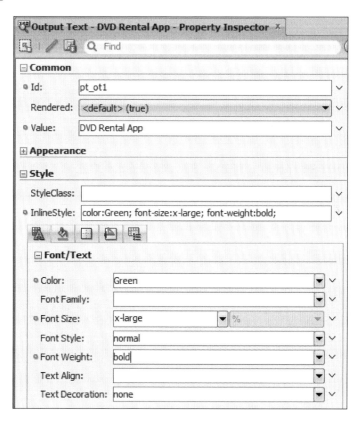

Creating Task Flows and Pages

You should see your choices reflected in the page template like this:

Example application

Now that we have templates for our page fragments and pages, it is time to start building the application itself.

Building the customer search page

To build the customer search screen, we refer back to the wireframe:

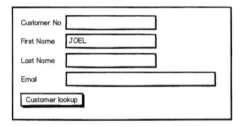

Starting from the `return-dvd-flow` task flow, double-click on the `findCustomer` view to create the ADF page fragment. You can leave the name and other settings, but select to use the `pageFragmentTemplate` as shown in the following screenshot:

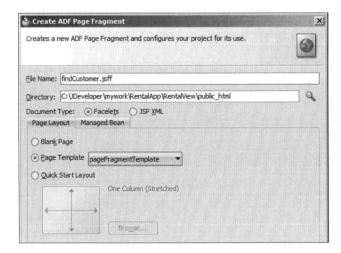

Because we need to place multiple input fields on the screen, it's a good idea to start with a **panel form layout**. Choose this from the **Component Palette** (from the **Layout** section). Inside the panel form layout, place four **Input Text** components (from the **Text and Selection** section). Use the **Property Palette** to provide labels.

> We are again hard-wiring text in—if you might need to translate the user interface later, use resource bundles as described earlier in this chapter.

Also, set the **Value** property to the correct variable (`#{pageFlowScope.searchCustomerId}`, `#{pageFlowScope.searchEmail}`, `#{pageFlowScope.searchFirstName}`, or `#{pageFlowScope.searchLastName}`—remember, we decided on these names when we dropped the `ExecuteWithParams` element onto the task flow). Your screen should look like this:

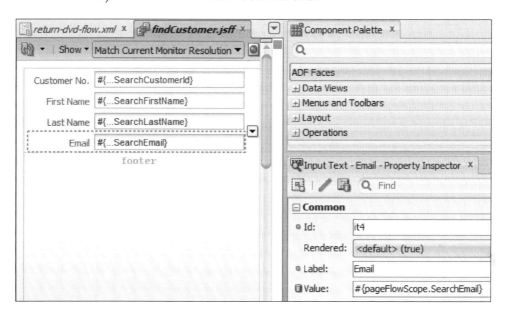

Now you have some fields for the user to enter query criteria. We have set the **Value** properties, in effect defining `pageFlowScope` variables. Later in the flow, we will assign the values of these variables to bind variables in a query in order to limit the records shown on a later screen.

Creating Task Flows and Pages

After the input fields, drop a **Button** component (from the **General Controls** section) onto the footer facet of the panel form layout (marked with the text **footer**), as shown in the following screenshot:

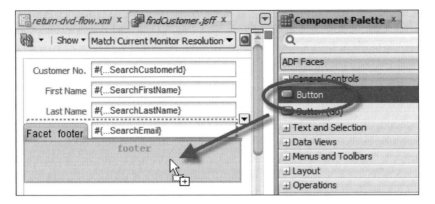

Use the **Property Inspector** to set the button **Text property** to **Customer lookup** and choose executeQuery as the **Action** as shown in the following screenshot:

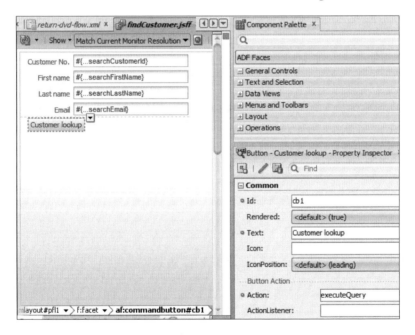

The possibilities in the drop-down for the **Action** property are the control flows you defined pointing away from the page fragment in the task flow.

Building the Return DVD page

The Return DVD page must contain both a master section showing customer information and a detail table showing all the non-returned DVDs for that customer. However, JDeveloper can automatically create all the necessary components for us at the same time as we define the data binding. So for now, simply double-click on the `showRentals` view in the task flow, ensure that `pageFragmentTemplate` is selected, and click on **OK**.

This creates an empty page for us to use later in this chapter when we finalize the application by building the model layer.

An alternative – ADF query panel

In this application, we are explicitly using a search page, a query operation, and a results page. However, ADF also offers the possibility to create a query panel and a result table on the same page. If you want to try out this component, you can create an empty page and drag the `CustomerVOCriteria` node (under the **Named Criteria** heading) onto a page and select **Query** | **ADF Query Panel with Table** as shown in the following screenshot:

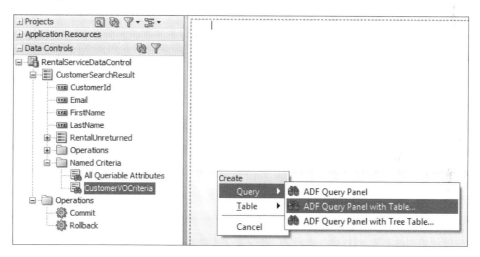

Building the Rent DVD page

The page to rent a DVD is so simple that we did not even create a wireframe for it. The use case is that a store employee will hold a specific DVD in their hand that the customer has selected and can read the `inventory_id` directly from a label on the DVD cover. Similarly, the customer will have a membership card containing `customer_id`. So, this simple screen just needs two input fields for these numbers and a button to register the rental.

Creating Task Flows and Pages

For now, we will just create the user interface—the logic to actually insert a rental record in the database will be added in *Chapter 4, Adding Business Logic*.

Open the `rent-dvd-flow` task flow and double-click on the `rentDvd` view. In the **Create ADF Page Fragment** dialog, ensure that `pageFragmentTemplate` is selected and click on **OK**.

This page will contain fields and a button just like the `findCustomer` page fragment, so it is built in a similar manner:

1. Add `PanelFormLayout`.
2. Add two fields to the panel form layout and set the labels.
3. Add a button to the footer facet of the panel form layout and set the label.

Your screen should look like this:

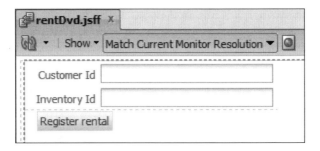

Building a master page

We now have two task flows using page fragments, but we cannot directly run task flows with page fragments. In order to run the application, we need to create a master page. In this sample application, we will just place the two task flows side by side on a page, but you could also use a menu and a dynamic region to swap between the rent and return flows.

To create the page, choose **File** | **New** | **Web Tier** | **JSF/Facelets** | **Page**. Give your page the name `simpleDvdStore.jsf`, select **Facelets** as **Document Type**, and select the `pageTemplate` we created earlier in the chapter. When you click on **OK**, you should see your page showing the header from the page template. In the **Structure** panel, you can see that the page contains a page template, and within the template, you can see the `pageContent` facet you defined, like this:

Chapter 3

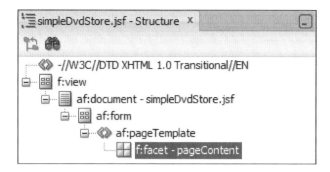

Drag a **Panel Splitter** (from the **Layout** section) onto the content facet in the **Structure** panel. This component splits an area into two separate parts (vertically or horizontally), dividing them with a movable splitter bar. In the **Design** view, you'll see a small button with a triangle, indicating the splitter bar in the panel splitter component. Drag the `rent-dvd-flow` task flow onto the left-hand side of the `simpleDvdStore` page and drop it as a region as shown in the following screenshot:

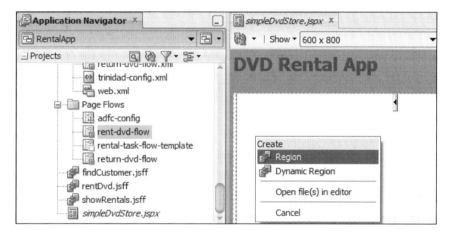

Move the splitter a bit to the right so you can see the full length of the fields. The first page from the flow is shown on the page, but it is grayed out to indicate that the components are not actually on the page, but rather come from a task flow.

[111]

Creating Task Flows and Pages

Next, drop the `return-dvd-flow` task flow on to the right-hand side of the screen as a region. Your screen should now look like this:

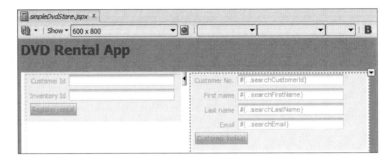

Note that both sides of the splitter should show a grayed-out version of the first page in each task flow. If you are reading this book in paper format, the above illustration might not exactly illustrate this grayed-out text.

Running the page

We are finally able to run our application! As discussed in *Chapter 1, My First ADF Essentials Application,* running your application is much faster in the WebLogic application server built into JDeveloper, so we'll do that here. Right-click on the `simpleDvdStore` page and choose **Run**. In the **Log** window at the bottom of the JDeveloper window, you will see the WebLogic server starting, and after a while, you should see your page:

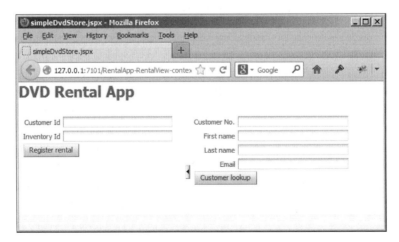

To run your application in GlassFish, you need to perform the tasks mentioned at the end of *Chapter 1*, *My First ADF Essentials Application*, configure datasource deployment, fix `bc4j.xcfg`, set the platform, and deploy.

Using data bindings

The final layer in the ADF model-view-controller architecture is the model layer. In ADF, the model layer is implemented in the ADF bindings that connect the view and controller layer to the underlying business services. The business services are presented as data controls—if you define ADF Business Components in JDeveloper, you automatically get a data control for each application module. However, it is also possible to manually create data controls based on Plain Old Java Objects (POJOs), web services, or other sources.

In your first Oracle ADF applications, you will probably not be interacting much with the binding layer. This is not necessary, because JDeveloper offers excellent support for "automagically" creating components from data controls, including establishing all the necessary bindings. Let's see this JDeveloper magic in action.

Showing a customer on a page

Now is the time to return to the `showRentals` page fragment that we skipped in the previous section. Open the page fragment from the **Application Navigator** or from the `return-dvd-flow` task flow.

Next, open the **Data Controls** panel in the **Application Navigator** and expand the `RentalServiceDataControl` node to see `CustomerSearchResult`. Drag the `CustomerSearchResult` element onto the page fragment and drop it as an ADF form as shown in the following screenshot:

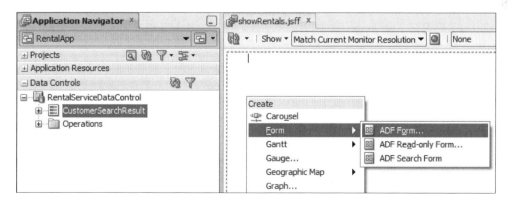

Creating Task Flows and Pages

In the **Edit Form Fields** dialog, check the **Include Navigation Controls** checkbox at the bottom of the dialog and click on OK. You will see JDeveloper automatically adding fields and buttons to the page. The **Structure** panel gives you an overview of what was just created for you:

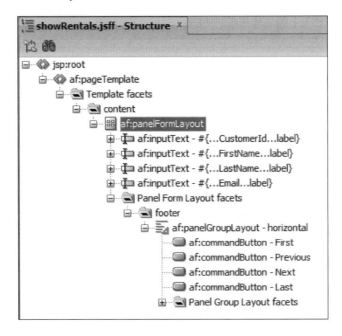

There is an `af:panelFormLayout` component and some fields, just like we created ourselves earlier, as well as some buttons in the footer facet of the panel form layout arranged in a horizontal layout within an `af:panelGroupLayout` container.

If you examine the fields, you will see that their **Label** property is set to something that starts with #{bindings—for example, the `CustomerId` field has the **Label** `#{bindings.CustomerId.hints.label}`. The **Value** property is set similarly—for example, the `CustomerId` field has the **Value** `#{bindings.CustomerId.inputValue}`.

What does this mean? Well, to get an explanation, you have to click on the **Bindings** tab at the bottom of the `showRentals.jsff` window. You will see a graphical representation of the binding layer like this:

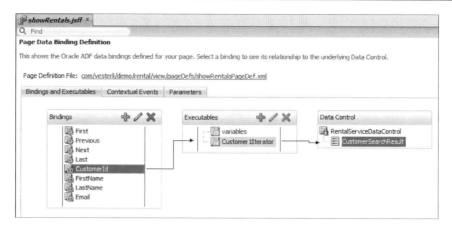

The use of the binding layer is an intermediate ADF topic that you will learn more about as you gain experience with ADF. For now, you can see that JDeveloper has created **attributeValues** bindings that point to an iterator that again points to the data control. This allows the user interface to access the **UI Hint** from the entity object or view object to use as a default label and to access the actual attribute value to display in the field.

 An iterator is a pointer to the current row in the dataset that the view object represents.

Similarly, there are action bindings that point to the same iterator.

If you go back to the **Design** view of the page and click on one of the buttons (for example, the `First` button), you can see in the **Property Inspector** that the `ActionListener` property also points to the binding layer. For example, the **Action Listener** for the `First` button is set to `#{bindings.First.execute}`, which means that it will execute the action binding called `First`. This action binding connects to the `Customer1Iterator` where it will execute the `First` operation, jumping to the first record in the record set.

 These actions move the iterator to point to the first record in the dataset of the view. The other operations move the iterator as their name implies.

Creating Task Flows and Pages

There is no need for you to change anything - you just need to save the `showRentals` page fragment. JDeveloper has worked its magic, and your application is actually ready to run without you writing a single line of code. Right-click on `simpleDvdStore.jsf` in the **Application Navigator** and choose **Run** to start your application. Your application should look like this:

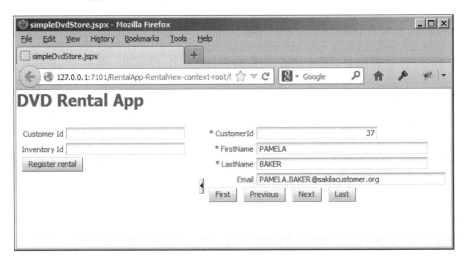

The default field labels come from the data binding (from the entity object or view object), but you can override the defaults by explicitly setting the **Label** property.

On the right-hand side, where the `return-dvd-flow` task flow lives within its region, you can type, for example, BA into the **Last Name** field and click on the **Customer Lookup** button. Only the right-hand side of the page changes to show you the second page fragment in the task flow – that's the one where we just dropped an ADF form based on a customer. You can click on the buttons to navigate through all the customers where the last name contains BA.

You'll see both BAKER and LOMBARDI because the view criteria defined on the view object used the `Contains` operator. You could also create the view criteria using, for example, the `Starts with` operator.

Showing customer rentals on a page

We have seen that we can find the right customers, but the wireframe indicated that we also need to show their non-returned rentals. To achieve this, we first need to change the layout of the page to make room for a table of rentals below the customers and then place the actual rental table on the page.

Chapter 3

To change the layout, right-click on `af:panelFormLayout` in the **Structure** panel and choose **Surround With**. Select a **Panel Group Layout** from the dialog and click on **OK**. In the **Property Inspector**, set the **Layout** property of the newly created panel group layout to **Vertical**. Also, set the **StyleClass** property to `AFStretchWidth`. This is a built-in CSS style that tells ADF to render the component across all available space.

We can't just drop the customer table onto the panel form layout. The First/Previous/Next/Last buttons are in the footer facet of the panel form layout, so they are always shown below the entire content of the panel form layout. Instead, we just wrapped the panel form layout in a vertical panel group layout so we can place the customer table below the entire panel form layout (buttons and all).

Now expand the `CustomerSearchResult` node in the **Data Controls** panel, find the `RentalUnreturned` element, and drag it onto the page below the buttons. In the **Create** pop-up menu, choose **Table | ADF Table**. In the **Edit Table Columns** dialog, remove all the `XxxId` columns (`RentalId`, `InventoryId`, and so on) as well as the `LastUpdate` and `ReturnDate` columns. Set **Row Selection** to **Single Row** and check the checkbox **Enable Sorting** to allow the user to sort rentals by clicking on column headers. Finally, sort the columns in the following order:

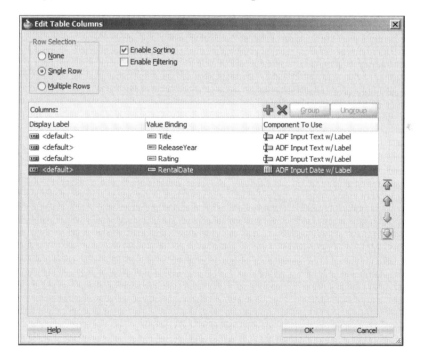

Next, click on **OK**. JDeveloper now places a table on the `showRentals` page fragment, but you need to change a few things to make the table expand nicely across all available space:

1. Select the `af:table` component in the **Structure** panel, and in the **Property Inspector**, set the StyleClass property to `AFStretchWidth` in order to make the table fill all available space.
2. Click on the **Title** column and find the value for `Id` (typically something like `c1`). Then, select the table in the **Property Inspector**, and in the `ColumnStretching` property (in the **Appearance** section), select the value corresponding to the **Title** column (for example, `column:c1`). This tells ADF to use any extra space for the **Title** column.

Your application should now look like this:

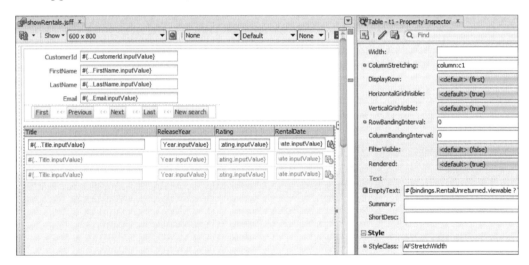

Chapter 3

Now right-click on `simpleDvdStore.jspx` and choose **Run** to run the application again. You will now see a table of unreturned rentals for the current customer as shown in the following screenshot:

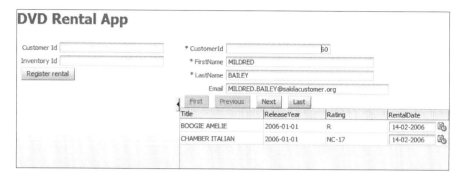

Because we created a view link between customers and unreturned rentals (in *Chapter 2, Creating Business Services*), ADF automatically takes care of the master-detail navigation. Whenever you use the buttons to move between customers, ADF automatically refreshes the table showing the unreturned rentals for that specific customer. Remember that you will only find unreturned DVDs if you updated the Sakila database from the default as described in *Chapter 1, My First ADF Essentials Application*.

Notice a cool feature of the ADF splitter component we use: if you click on the little triangle, the left-hand side is collapsed, and the right-hand side automatically takes over this space. The **Title** column will take over the extra space because of the `ColumnStretching` property. Also note that you can sort the table by clicking on the column titles, and you can resize and even reorder the columns. The ADF table component is pretty awesome!

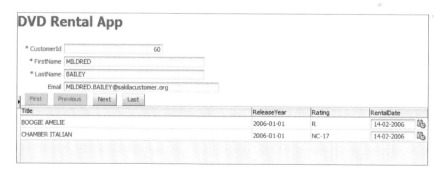

[119]

Adding navigation

The final thing missing from the application is the navigation back to the customer search. This is really simple to add—just drag a button from the **Component Palette** and drop it to the right of the Last button (inside the panel group layout box). Use the **Property Inspector** to set the **Text** property to New search and select newSearch as **Action** (the name of the navigation flow away from showRentals). Run your application again and verify that the **New search** button takes you back to the customerSearch page fragment.

> Notice that the left-hand side of the screen is not repainted even though you navigate between page fragments in the right-hand side. This is one of the powerful features of ADF, called **Partial Page Rendering**—only the parts of the screen that change need to be redrawn.

Summary

We have now built a good part of the application and can search and navigate through records, including master-detail relationships. And we still haven't written a single line of code. Have you seen enough declarative development? And are you itching to start writing code? Quickly, on to the next chapter!

4
Adding Business Logic

So far, we have only been using the declarative power of JDeveloper and the ADF framework. The application you saw running in the last chapter did not contain a single line of hand-written code. Of course, declarative features can only get you so far -- once you need to add the real-life business rules that are specific to your application, you will have to start writing Java code.

This chapter will give you some examples of this — many other examples are available on the Internet. At the end of the chapter, we will see how to implement the business logic necessary for the DVD rental application.

If you are using Google to search for code snippets, always start by searching only for results from within the past year (navigate to **Search Tools** and change the **Any time** default setting to **Past year**). A search without a date range is likely to show up old solutions, and a lot of things have got easier in the later versions of JDeveloper.

Adding logic to business components

As you saw in *Chapter 2, Creating Business Services*, by default, a business component does not have an explicit Java class. When you want to add Java logic, however, you generate the relevant Java class from the **Java** tab of the business component.

On the **Java** tab, you also decide which of your methods are to be made available to other objects by choosing to implement a **Client Interface**. Methods that implement a client interface show up in the **Data Control** palette and can be called from outside the object.

Adding Business Logic

Logic in entity objects

Remember from *Chapter 2, Creating Business Services*, that entity objects are closest to your database tables -- most often, you will have one entity object for every table in the database. This makes the entity object a good place to put data logic that must be always executed. If you place, for example, validation logic in an entity object, it will be applied no matter which view object attempts to change data.

> **In the database or in an entity object?**
>
> Much of the business logic you can place in an entity object can also be placed in the database using database triggers. If other systems are accessing your database tables, business logic should go into the database as much as possible.

Overriding accessors

To use Java in entity objects, you open an entity object and select the **Java** tab. When you click on the pencil icon, the **Select Java Options** dialog opens as shown in the following screenshot:

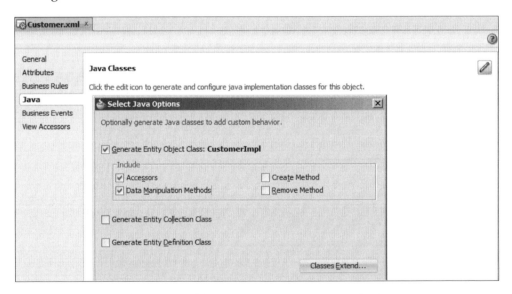

In this dialog, you can select to generate **Accessors** (the setXxx() and getXxx() methods for all the attributes) as well as **Data Manipulation Methods** (the doDML() method; there is more on this later).

Chapter 4

When you click on **OK**, the entity object class is generated for you. You can open it by clicking on the hyperlink or you can find it in the **Application Navigator** panel as a new node under the entity object. If you look inside this file, you will find:

- Your class should start with an `import` section that contains a statement that imports your `EntityImpl` class. If you have set up your framework extension classes correctly (as described in *Chapter 2, Creating Business Services*), this could be `import com.adfessentials.adf.framework.EntityImpl`. You will have to click on the plus sign in the left margin to expand the import section.

- The **Structure** panel in the bottom-left shows an overview of the class including all the methods it contains. You will see a lot of setter and getter methods like `getFirstName()` and `setFirstName()` as shown in the following screenshot:

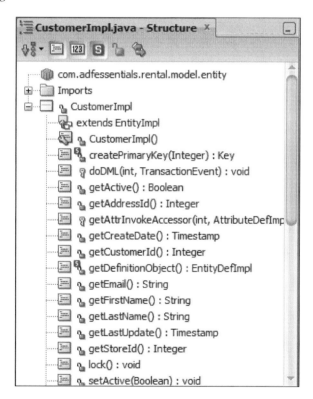

- There is a `doDML()` method described later.

Adding Business Logic

If you were to decide, for example, that last name should always be stored in upper case, you could change the `setLastName()` method to:

```
public void setLastName(String value) {
  setAttributeInternal(LASTNAME, value.toUpperCase());
}
```

Working with database triggers

If you decide to keep some of your business logic in database triggers, your triggers might change the values that get passed from the entity object. Because the entity object caches values to save database work, you need to make sure that the entity object stays in sync with the database even if a trigger changes a value. You do this by using the **Refresh on Update** property.

To find this property, select the **Attributes** subtab on the left and then select the attribute that might get changed. At the bottom of the screen, you see various settings for the attribute with the **Refresh** settings in the top-right of the **Details** tab as shown in the following screenshot:

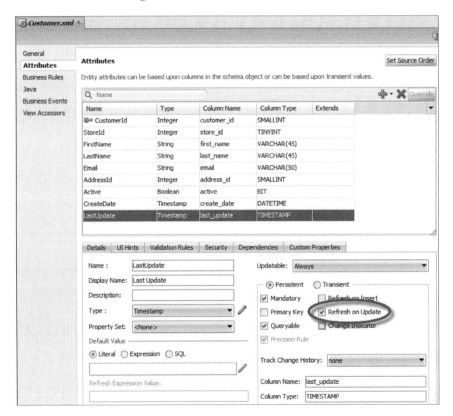

Check the **Refresh on Update** property checkbox if a database trigger might change the attribute value. This makes the ADF framework requery the database after an update has been issued.

> **Refresh on Insert** doesn't work if you are using MySQL and your primary key is generated with `AUTO_INCREMENT` or set by a trigger. ADF doesn't know the primary key and therefore cannot find the newly inserted row after inserting it. It does work if you are running against an Oracle database, because Oracle SQL syntax has a special `RETURNING` construct that allows the entity object to get the newly created primary key back.

Overriding doDML()

Next, after the setters and getters, the `doDML()` method is the one that most often gets overridden. This method is called whenever an entity object wants to execute a **Data Manipulation Language** (**DML**) statement like `INSERT`, `UPDATE`, or `DELETE`. This offers you a way to add additional processing; for example, checking that the account balance is zero before allowing a customer to be deleted. In this case, you would add logic to check the account balance, and if the deletion is allowed, call `super.doDML()` to invoke normal processing.

Another example would be to implement logical delete (records only change state and are not actually deleted from the table). In this case, you would override `doDML()` as follows:

```
@override
protected void doDML(int operation, TransactionEvent e) {
  if (operation == DML_DELETE) {
    operation = DML_UPDATE;
  }
  super.doDML(operation, e);
}
```

As it is probably obvious from the code, this simply replaces a `DELETE` operation with an `UPDATE` before it calls the `doDML()` method of its superclass (your framework extension `EntityImpl`, which passes the task on to the Oracle-supplied `EntityImpl` class). Of course, you also need to change the state of the entity object row, for example, in the `remove()` method. You can find fully-functional examples of this approach on various blogs, for example at http://myadfnotebook.blogspot.dk/2012/02/updating-flag-when-deleting-entity-in.html.

Adding Business Logic

You also have the option of completely replacing normal doDML() method processing by simply not calling super.doDML(). This could be the case if you want all your data modifications to go via a database procedure -- for example, to insert an actor, you would have to call insertActor with first name and last name. In this case, you would write something like:

```
@override
protected void doDML(int operation, TransactionEvent e) {
  CallableStatement cstmt = null;
  if (operation == DML_INSERT) {
    String insStmt = "{call insertActor (?,?)}";
    cstmt = getDBTransaction().createCallableStatement(insStmt,
      0);
    try {
      cstmt.setString(1, getFirstName());
      cstmt.setString(2, getLastName());
      cstmt.execute();
    }
    catch (Exception ex) {
      ...
    } finally {
      ...
    }
  }
}
```

If the operation is insert, the above code uses the current transaction (via the getDBTransaction() method) to create a CallableStatement with the string insertActor(?,?). Next, it binds the two parameters (indicated by the question marks in the statement string) to the values for first name and last name (by calling the getter methods for these two attributes). Finally, the code block finishes with a normal catch clause to handle SQL errors and a finally clause to close open objects. Again, fully working examples are available in the documentation and on the Internet in various blog posts.

Normally, you would implement this kind of override in the framework extension EntityImpl class, with additional logic to allow the framework extension class to recognize which specific entity object the operation applies to and which database procedure to call.

Data validation

With the techniques you have just seen, you can implement every kind of business logic your requirements call for. One requirement, however, is so common that it has been built right into the ADF framework: **data validation**.

Declarative validation

The simplest kind of validation is where you compare one individual attribute to a limit, a range, or a number of fixed values. For this kind of validation, no code is necessary at all. You simply select the **Business Rules** subtab in the entity object, select an attribute, and click on the green plus sign to add a validation rule. The **Add Validation Rule** dialog appears as shown in the following screenshot:

You have a number of options for **Rule Type** -- depending on your choice here, the **Rule Definition** tab changes to allow you to define the parameters for the rule.

Adding Business Logic

On the **Failure Handling** tab, you can define whether the validation is an error (that must be corrected) or a warning (that the user can override), and you define a message text as shown in the following screenshot:

You can even define variable **message tokens** by using curly brackets { } in your message text. If you do so, a token will automatically be added to the **Token Message Expressions** section of the dialog, where you can assign it any value using Expression Language. Click on the **Help** button in the dialog for more information on this.

> If your application might ever conceivably be needed in a different language, use the looking glass icon to define a resource string stored in a separate resource bundle. This allows your application to have multiple resource bundles, one for each different user interface language.

There is also a **Validation Execution** tab that allows you to specify under which condition your rule should be applied. This can be useful if your logic is complex and resource intensive. If you do not enter anything here, your rule is always executed.

Regular expression validation

One of the especially powerful declarative validations is the **Regular Expression** validation. A regular expression is a very compact notation that can define the format of a string -- this is very useful for checking e-mail addresses, phone numbers, and so on. To use this, set **Rule Type** to **Regular Expression** as shown in the following screenshot:

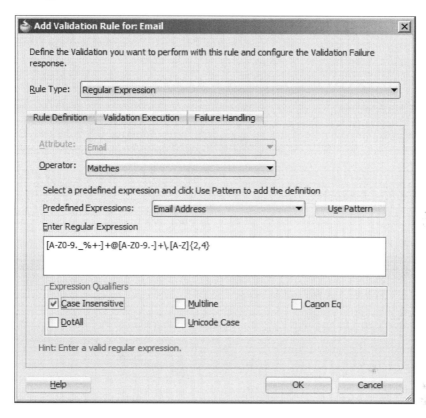

JDeveloper offers you a few predefined regular expressions, for example, the validation for e-mails as shown in the preceding screenshot.

> Even though you can find lots of predefined regular expressions on the Internet, someone from your team should understand the basics of regular expression syntax so you can create the exact expression you need.

Groovy scripts

You can also set **Rule Type** to **Script** to get a free-format box where you can write a **Groovy** expression. Groovy is a scripting language for the Java platform that works well together with Java -- see `http://groovy.codehaus.org/` for more information on Groovy.

 Oracle has published a white paper on Groovy in ADF (`http://www.oracle.com/technetwork/developer-tools/jdev/introduction-to-groovy-128837.pdf`), and there is also information on Groovy in the JDeveloper help.

Method validation

If none of these methods for data validation fit your need, you can of course always revert to writing code. To do this, set **Rule Type** to **Method** and provide an error message. If you leave the **Create a Select Method** checkbox checked when you click on **OK**, JDeveloper will automatically create a method with the right signature and add it to the Java class for the entity object. The autogenerated validation method for `Length` (in the `Film` entity object) would look as follows:

```
/**
 * Validation method for Length.
 */
public boolean validateLength (Integer length) {
   return true;
}
```

It is your task to fill in the logic and return either `true` (if validation is OK) or `false` (if the data value does not meet the requirements). If validation fails, ADF will automatically display the message you defined for this validation rule.

Logic in view objects

View objects represent the dataset you need for a specific part of the application — typically a specific screen or part of a screen. You can create Java objects for either an entire view object (an `XxxImpl.java` class, where `Xxx` is the name of your view object) or for a specific row (an `XxxRowImpl.java` class).

A view object class contains methods to work with the entire data-set that the view object represents -- for example, methods to apply view criteria or re-execute the underlying database query. The view row class contains methods to work with an individual record of data -- mainly methods to set and get attribute values for one specific record.

Overriding accessors

Like for entity objects, you can override the accessors (setters and getters) for view objects. To do this, you use the **Java** subtab in the view object and click on the pencil icon next to **Java Classes** to generate Java. You can select to generate a view row class including accessors to ask JDeveloper to create a view row implementation class as shown in the following screenshot:

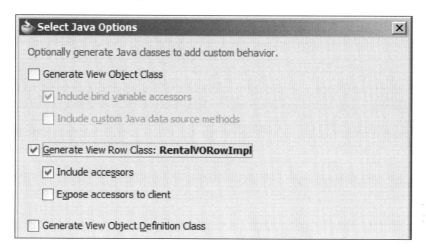

This will create an `XxxRowImpl` class (for example, `RentalVORowImpl`) with setter and getter methods for all attributes. The code will look something like the following code snippet:

```
...
public class RentalVORowImpl extends ViewRowImpl {
...
/**
 * This is the default constructor (do not remove).
 */
  public RentalVORowImpl() {
  }

...
  /**
   * Gets the attribute value for title using the alias name
   * Title.
   * @return the title
   */
  public String getTitle() {
    return (String) getAttributeInternal(TITLE);
```

Adding Business Logic

```
    }
    /**
     * Sets <code>value</code> as attribute value for title using
     * the alias name Title.
     * @param value value to set the title
     */
    public void setTitle(String value) {
      setAttributeInternal(TITLE, value);
    }
    ...
}
```

You can change all of these to manipulate data before it is delivered to the entity object or to return a processed version of an attribute value. At the end of this chapter, we will use this method for a transient attribute that is not mapped to an entity object. To use such attributes, you can write code in the implementation class to determine which value to return.

> You can also use Groovy expressions to determine values for transient attributes. This is done on the **Value** subtab for the attribute by setting **Value Type** to **Expression** and filling in the **Value** field with a Groovy expression. See the Oracle white paper on Groovy in ADF (`http://www.oracle.com/technetwork/developer-tools/jdev/introduction-to-groovy-128837.pdf`) or the JDeveloper help.

Change view criteria

Another example of coding in a view object is to dynamically change which view criteria are applied to the view object. You saw in *Chapter 2, Creating Business Services*, that it is possible to define many view criteria on a view object -- when you add a view object instance to an application module, you decide which of the available view criteria to apply to that specific view object instance.

However, you can also programmatically change which view criteria are applied to a view object. This can be useful if you want to have buttons to control which subset of data to display -- in the example application, you could imagine a button to "show only overdue rentals" that would apply an extra view criterion to a rental view object.

Because the view criteria apply to the whole dataset, view criteria methods go into the view object, not the view row object. You generate a Java class for the view object from the **Java Options** dialog in the same way as you generate Java for the view row object. In the **Java Options** dialog, select the option to generate the view object class as shown in the following screenshot:

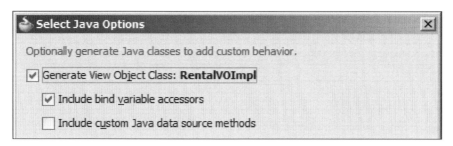

A simple example of programmatically applying a view criteria would be a method to apply an already defined view criterion called called `OverdueCriterion` to a view object. This would look like this in the view object class:

```
public void showOnlyOverdue() {
   ViewCriteria vc = getViewCriteria("OverdueCriterion");
   applyViewCriteria(vc);
   executeQuery();
}
```

View criteria often have bind variables -- for example, you could have a view criteria called `OverdueByDaysCriterion` that uses a bind variable `OverdueDayLimit`. When you generate Java for the view object, the default option of **Include bind variable accessors** (shown in the preceding screenshot) will create a `setOverdueDayLimit()` method if you have an `OverdueDayLimit` bind variable.

A method in the view object to which we apply this criterion might look like the following code snippet:

```
public void showOnlyOverdueByDays(int days) {
   ViewCriteria vc = getViewCriteria("OverdueByDaysCriterion");
   setOverdueDayLimit(days);
   applyViewCriteria(vc);
   executeQuery();
}
```

If you want to call these methods from the user interface, you must select **create a client interface** for them (on the **Java** subtab in the view object). This will make your method available in the **Data Control** palette, ready to be dragged onto a page and dropped as a button.

Adding Business Logic

> When you change the view criteria and execute the query, only the content of the view object changes -- the screen does not automatically repaint itself. In order to ensure that the screen refreshes, you need to set the **PartialTriggers** property of the data table to point to the ID of the button that changes the view criteria. For more on partial page rendering, see the *Oracle Fusion Middleware Web User Interface Developer's Guide for Oracle Application Development Framework* (http://docs.oracle.com/cd/E37975_01/web.111240/e16181/af_ppr.htm).

Logic in application modules

You've now seen how to add logic to both entity objects and view objects. However, you can also add custom logic to application modules. An application module is the place where logic that does not belong to a specific view object goes -- for example, calls to stored procedures that involve data from multiple view objects.

To generate a Java class for an application module, you navigate to the **Java** subtab in the application module and select the pencil icon next to the **Java Classes** heading. Typically, you create Java only for the application module class and not for the application module definition.

You can also add your own logic here that gets called from the user interface or you can override the existing methods in the application module. A typical method to override is prepareSession(), which gets called before the application module establishes a connection to the database -- if you need to, for example, call stored procedures or do other kinds of initialization before accessing the database, an application module method is a good place to do so. Remember that you need to define your own methods as client methods on the **Java** tab of the application module for the method to be available to be called from elsewhere in the application.

Because the application module handles the transaction, it also contains methods, such as beforeCommit(), beforeRollback(), afterCommit(), afterRollback(), and so on.

> The doDML() method on any entity object that is part of the transaction is executed before any of the application modules' methods.

Adding logic to the user interface

Logic in the user interface is implemented in the form of managed beans. These are Java classes that are registered with the task flow and automatically instantiated by the ADF framework. As you might remember from *Chapter 3, Creating Task Flows and Pages*, ADF operates with various memory scopes -- you have to decide on a scope when you define a managed bean.

Adding a bean method to a button

The simplest way to add logic to the user interface is to drop a button (`af:commandButton`) onto a page or page fragment and then double-click on it. This brings up the **Bind Action Property** dialog as shown in the following screenshot:

If you leave **Method Binding** selected and click on **New**, the **Create Managed Bean** dialog appears as shown in the following screenshot:

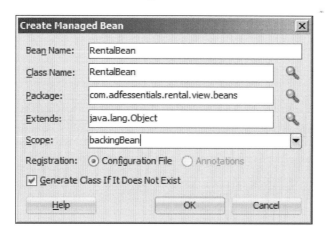

Adding Business Logic

In this dialog, you can give your bean a name, provide a class name (typically the same as the bean name), and select a scope. The `backingBean` scope is a good scope for logic that is only used for one action when the user clicks on the button and which does not need to store any state for later. Leaving the **Generate Class If It Does Not Exist** checkbox checked asks JDeveloper to create the class for you. When you click on **OK**, JDeveloper will automatically suggest a method for you in the **Method** dropdown (based on the ID of the button you double-clicked on). In the **Method** field, provide a more useful name and click on **OK** to add the new class and open it in the editor. You will see a method with your chosen name, as shown in the following code snippet:

```
Public String rentDvd() {
  // Add event code here...
  return null;
}
```

Obviously, you place your code inside this method.

 If you accidentally left the default method name and ended up with something like `cb5_action()`, you can right-click on the method name and navigate to **Refactor** | **Rename** to give it a more descriptive name.

Note that JDeveloper automatically sets the **Action** property for your button matching the scope, bean name, and method name. This might be something like `#{backingBeanScope.RentalBean.rentDvd}`.

Adding a bean to a task flow

Your beans should always be part of a task flow. If you're not adding logic to a button, or you just want more control over the process, you can also create a backing bean class first and then add it to the task flow.

A bean class is a regular Java class created by navigating to **File** | **New** | **Java Class**.

When you have created the class, you open the task flow where you want to use it and select the **Overview** tab. On the **Managed Beans** subtab, you can use the green plus to add your bean. Simply give it a name, point to the class you created, and select a memory scope.

Accessing UI components from beans

In a managed bean, you often want to refer to various user interface elements. This is done by mapping each element to a property in the bean.

For example, if you have an `af:inputText` component that you want to refer to in a bean, you create a private variable of type `RichInputText` in the bean (with setter and getter methods) and set the **Binding** property (under the **Advanced** heading) to point to that bean variable using Expression Language. We'll see this method used in the example application at the end of this chapter.

When creating a page or page fragment, you have the option (on the **Managed Bean** tab) to automatically have JDeveloper create corresponding attributes for you. The **Managed Bean** tab is shown in the following screenshot:

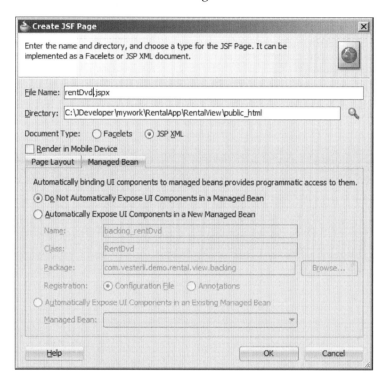

Leave it on the default setting of **Do Not Automatically Expose UI Components in a Managed Bean**. If you select one of the options to automatically expose UI elements, your bean will acquire a lot of attributes that you don't need, which will make your code unnecessarily complex and slow. However, while learning ADF, you might want to try this out to see how the bean attributes and the **Binding** property work together.

Adding Business Logic

 If you do activate this setting, it applies to every page and fragment you create until you explicitly deselect this option.

Accessing the binding layer

While the preceding method gives you access to all the user interface elements shown on the page, you will often need to access other data in order to make a decision. To do this, you need to programmatically access the binding layer.

 If you are familiar with JDBC but not yet familiar with data bindings, you might be tempted to write JDBC to directly access the database. Do not do this! It violates the separation of layers in the **Model-view-controller (MVC)** pattern, makes your code hard to maintain and might introduce subtle bugs when your bean accesses the values in the database, but the user interface is working on non-committed data.

The first part of accessing the binding layer is always to get a `BindingContainer`. You do this with the following code:

```
BindingContainer bc = 
  BindingContext.getCurrent().getCurrentBindingsEntry();
```

You want your class to import the `oracle.binding.BindingContainer` interface and the `oracle.adf.model.BindingContext` class -- JDeveloper will normally prompt you for these imports.

Working with attribute values

If you want to access the value of an attribute, you first need to get a handle to the attribute binding as done in the following code snippet:

```
AttributeBinding ab = 
  (AttributeBinding)bc.getControlBinding("AttrName");
```

Then you can retrieve the value with `attr.getInputValue()` and set it with `attr.setInputValue()`.

This only works if such an attribute binding already exists. From the page where you are using the bean, you can click on the **Bindings** tab to see the existing attribute bindings (in the left-hand **Bindings** box), as shown in the following screenshot:

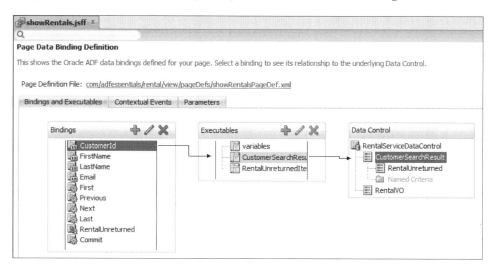

The preceding screenshot shows attribute bindings for `CustomerId`, `FirstName`, `LastName`, and `Email`. If you drop individual attributes from a view object instance on a page, JDeveloper creates a binding for that specific attribute -- if you drop a whole view object instance as an ADF form, JDeveloper will automatically create attribute bindings for all the attributes you select. If you don't see the attribute binding you need, you can add it with the green plus in the **Bindings** box.

Working with operations

If you want to work with operations on your data controls, you must first get a handle to the operations binding, as done in the following code snippet:

```
OperationBinding ob =
  bc.getOperationBinding("OprName");
```

Then, you can execute the operation with `ob.execute()`.

If your operation takes parameters, you can call `getParamsMap()` to get a map object that you can populate with parameter names and values before calling `execute()`.

Like for attribute bindings, this only works if the operation you want to call is already defined in your binding context. The preceding screenshot shows operation bindings for the **First**, **Previous**, **Next**, and **Last** built-in methods that a data control always has. Like for attribute bindings, you can add operation bindings by clicking on the green plus sign.

Working with whole datasets

If you want to work with more than just a single value, you need to access data through an **iterator**. To get a handle to the iterator, you first need to cast your binding container object to a DCBindingContainer, as shown in the following code snippet:

```
DCBindingContainer dcb = (DCBindingContainer)bc;
```

 Technically, BindingContainer is a Java interface, not a class. So, when you used the business component object earlier, you were actually using a JUFormBinding class implementing the BindingContainer interface.

Once you have the DCBindingContainer, you can retrieve the actual iterator with code, as shown in the following code snippet:

```
DCIteratorBinding iter = (DCIteratorBinding)
  dcb.findIteratorBinding("IterName");
```

This iterator object has the following methods to work on the dataset:

- getCurrentRow() returns a Row object for the current row.
- getAllRowsInRange() returns an array of Row objects representing all the rows that the iterator covers. Once you have this array, you can loop through it like any other array.

The Row objects have the getAttribute() and setAttribute() methods you can use to retrieve and change attribute values.

Showing messages

At some point in your ADF application development, you will come across the need to display a message to the user. The simplest way to do this is to make use of the JSF FacesContext object. This object represents all of the contextual information about a request and is created automatically; you can read information from it and add information to it during your processing of the request, and JSF will automatically display any messages that you have placed in the context at the end of request processing.

To display a message, use code like the following:

```
FacesContext fctx = FacesContext.getCurrentInstance();
FacesMessage fm = new FacesMessage("Message text");
fm.setSeverity(FacesMessage.SEVERITY_WARN);
fctx.addMessage(null, fm);
```

There are various severity levels available for informational messages, warnings, and errors.

The first parameter in the `addMessage()` method can be used to place the message near a specific component. If you use `null` as done in the preceding code snippet, the message will simply be centered on the screen. To place it near a component, you need access to the UI component you want to place the message near. The process of getting a pointer to a specific UI component in a bean is the same as described in the subsection *Accessing UI components from beans* in the *Adding logic to the user interface* section:

1. You create a property in your bean of the right class (for example, `RichInputText` for an input field) with setter and getter methods.
2. You connect the UI component on the page to the bean attribute by setting the `Binding` property.

So, if you have defined a `FirstName` element in your bean class, created a `getFirstName()` getter and a `setFirstName()` setter, and connected it to a UI component, your message code would look as follows:

```
Fctx.addMessage(getFirstName().getClientId(fctx), fm);
```

This will place the message close to that specific UI component.

Example application

The simple DVD rental application that we are building needs programming in two places:

- To register a rental (create new record)
- To register a return (update an attribute value)

Adding Business Logic

Registering a rental

You probably remember from *Chapter 3, Creating Task Flows and Pages*, that registering a new rental is simply a matter of registering two data values when the store clerk presses a button. The screen is shown in the following screenshot:

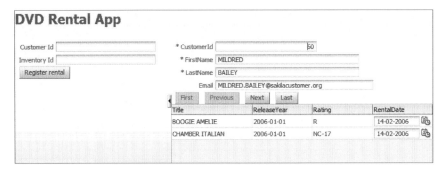

In this simple demo application, we are assuming that the clerk will read a customer ID from a membership card and an inventory ID from the cover of the DVD -- in a more user-friendly application, you could of course expand on this. But for now, we just need to insert a new record into the `Rental` table when the user has entered two values and pressed the button.

Creating a bean

Start by opening the **RentDvd** page fragment and double-clicking on the **Register rental** button. This brings up the **Bind Action Property** dialog where you can click on **New** to create a new managed bean. Give your bean the name `RentalBean`, class name `RentalBean`, provide a class name (by convention, beans are placed in their own `.beans` subpackage), and select the **backingBean** scope. The dialog should look as shown in the following screenshot:

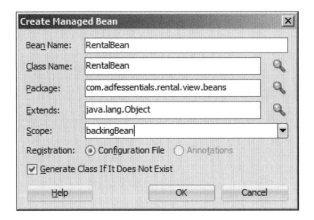

Click on **OK** to create the class. Change the method name to `rentDvd` (click inside the **Method** field and type the name; do not select the drop-down arrow) and click on **OK**. Your new bean class opens in the editor. Change to the tab showing the `rentDvd` page and verify that the **Action** property of the button is now `#{backingBeanScope.RentalBean.rentDvd}`.

Mapping the fields

Inside the bean, we need attributes matching the two fields on the screen and corresponding accessor methods. Add two attributes of type `RichInputText` called `customer` and `inventory`, right-click on the code, and click on **Generate Accessors** to generate setters and getters. Your code will look something like follows:

```
package com.vesterli.demo.rental.view.beans;

import ...

public class RentalBean {
  private RichInputText customer;
  private RichInputText inventory;

  public RentalBean() {
  }
  public String rentDvd() {
  }
  public void setCustomer(RichInputText customer) {
    this.customer = customer;
  }
  public RichInputText getCustomer() {
    return customer;
  }
  public void setInventory(RichInputText inventory) {
    this.inventory = inventory;
  }
  public RichInputText getInventory() {
    return inventory;
  }
}
```

Now the bean has two `RichInputText` attributes, but they are not connected to the actual input fields on the page yet. To do this, select the **Customer Id** field, navigate to the **Advanced** subtab, click on the little down arrow to the left of the **Binding** property, and click on **Edit**.

Adding Business Logic

In the **Edit Property** dialog, choose the **RentalBean** managed bean and the **customer** property from the dropdowns, as shown in the following screenshot:

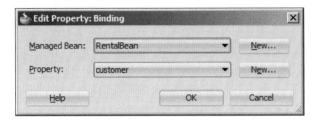

When you close this dialog, you should see the **Binding** property set to `#{backingBeanScope.RentalBean.customer}`.

In a similar way, connect the `Inventory Id` field to the `inventory` property.

Establishing bindings

We want our code to perform a database commit when the user clicks on the button, so we need to create a binding for the `Commit` operation from our data control.

Because we have not used the JDeveloper drag-and-drop features on this page at all, the `rentDVD.jsff` page fragment has no **Page Definition file**. To create one, right-click on the page fragment, click on **Go to Page Definition**, and answer **Yes** in the dialog asking you if you want to create this. The page definition for the page opens as shown in the following screenshot:

On this page, click on the green plus sign next to **Bindings** to create a new binding and click on **action** in the **Insert Item** dialog. The **Create Action Binding** dialog appears. Select the data control at the top and set **Operation** to **Commit** in the middle of the dialog as shown in the following screenshot:

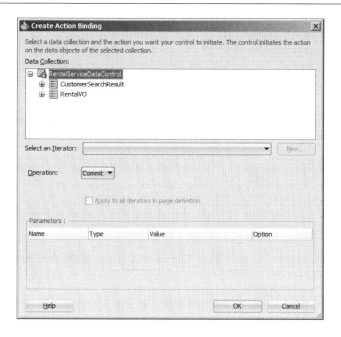

When you click on **OK**, an action binding is created for you.

All of this happens automatically when you drag the **Commit** operation onto a page from the data control. Because we just want the `Commit` action binding in order to call it programmatically (and not the button), we have to create the binding manually as shown in this section.

Next, we need an **Iterator** (a pointer to a specific record in the view object). Click on the green plus sign next to **Executables** and select **iterator**. In the **Create Iterator Binding** dialog, expand the data control, choose the `RentalVO` view object and click on **OK**. Your page bindings should now look as follows:

Adding Business Logic

Writing the code

The preceding procedure makes the value of the two fields available to the logic in the bean -- what remains is to add the actual insert in the `rentDvd()` method. Your code should look as follows:

```
public String rentDvd() {
  BindingContainer bc =
    BindingContext.getCurrent().getCurrentBindingsEntry();
  DCBindingContainer dcb = (DCBindingContainer)bc;
  DCIteratorBinding rentalIter =
    dcb.findIteratorBinding("RentalVOIterator");
  NameValuePairs attrib = new NameValuePairs();
  attrib.setAttribute("CustomerId", customer.getValue());
  attrib.setAttribute("InventoryId", inventory.getValue());
  //TODO: Look up user later when adding security
  attrib.setAttribute("StaffId", 1);
  attrib.setAttribute("RentalDate",
    new Timestamp(System.currentTimeMillis()));
  attrib.setAttribute("LastUpdate",
    new Timestamp(System.currentTimeMillis()));
  ViewObject rentalVO = rentalIter.getViewObject();
  rentalVO.createAndInitRow(attrib);
  OperationBinding ob = bc.getOperationBinding("Commit");
  ob.execute();
  return null;
}
```

As you write the code, you will be prompted for various imports that exist in several packages -- import `BindingContainer` from `oracle.binding`, `BindingContext` from `oracle.adf.model`, `Timestamp` from `java.sql`, and `OperationBinding` from `oracle.binding`.

You'll recognize the part about getting an iterator binding from earlier in this chapter.

The next part creates a `NameValuePairs` object that we need in order to call the `createAndInitRow()` method that actually creates the new record. Because the bean has a `customer` attribute, we can just use `customer.getValue()` to get the value that the user has entered into the `customer` field (and similarly for `inventory`). We must provide a Staff ID -- since we haven't added security yet, we'll just hardwire a constant in for now.

Next, we get the view object `rentalVO` from the iterator because the `createAndInitRow()` method we need to create a new view row is found on the `ViewObject` object.

Finally, we get the `Commit` binding and execute it in order to commit the transaction to the database.

Registering a return

We also need to be able to register when a customer returns a DVD. We didn't include this functionality in the user interface wireframe, so there is no button or other way to return a DVD yet.

There are at least three ways to allow the user to mark multiple rentals returned:

1. Add a checkbox to each row and a button to mark all checked rentals as returned. The logic behind the button would loop through the iterator and update all records where the checkmark is checked.

2. Use the ADF multi-select feature (the **RowSelection** property **multiple** on `af:table`) and a button. The button would use the `getSelectedRowKeys()` method on the `RichTable` object to retrieve the selected rows, look them up in the view object, and update them.

3. Add a button to each row, set **RowSelection single** to ensure that only one row is selected, and use `getSelectedRowKeys()` as above to update that one row.

Because we can't be sure the user realizes that they can do multi-select (the feature is not "discoverable" in user experience terminology), we don't want to do number 2. Number 1 is the typical way of doing multi-record operations in a web application, but option number 3 actually saves a click, so we'll go with that option.

Adding a column and a button

First, we need to add an extra column to the rentals table. Open the `showRentals.jsff` page fragment and find the `af:table` in the **Structure** panel (in the bottom-left corner of the JDeveloper window). Right-click on it and click on **Insert Inside af:table**, **Column**. This adds a blank column to your table. It should be added last (right-most) — if it isn't, grab it in the **Structure** panel and drag-and-drop it to be last in the table.

Select the column and set the **HeaderText** property to `Return`.

Adding Business Logic

Finally, drag a **Button** component from the **Component Palette** onto the newly created column and set the **Text** property for the button to Return. Your screen should now look as shown in the following screenshot:

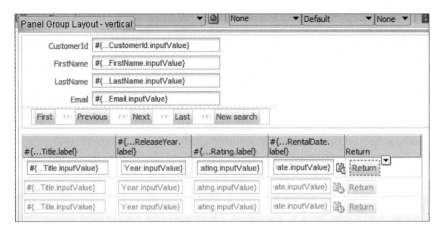

Creating a bean

To create a managed bean, you can double-click on the new **Return** button and click on **New** to create a new managed bean. Give it the name ReturnBean, class name ReturnBean, provide a class name, and select the backingBean scope. Click on **OK** and give the method the name returnDvd.

Mapping the table

In this bean, we need a table property in order to retrieve the selected record, so you need to add a RichTable attribute with the name **filmRentalTable** and create a setter and getter (right-click on **Generate Accessors**). Your code will look something like as shown in the following code snippet:

```
package com.vesterli.demo.rental.view.beans;

import ...

public class ReturnBean {
  private RichTable filmRentalTable;

  public RentalBean() {
  }
  public String returnDvd() {
```

```
      }
      public void setFilmRentalTable (RichTable filmRentalTable) {
        this.filmRentalTable = filmRentalTable;
      }
      public RichTable getFilmRentalTable () {
        return filmRentalTable;
      }
    }
```

Connect the `RichTable` property to `ReturnBean` by returning to the showRentals page fragment and setting the **Binding** property of the table to #{backingBeanScope.ReturnBean.filmRentalTable}.

Creating a view object method

To illustrate how to add logic to the business components, we will add a method called `registerReturn()` to the `RentalVO` view row object. To generate the Java class where our method goes, open the model project and then the `RentalVO` view object, navigate to the **Java** tab, and click on the pencil icon next to **Java Classes** to open the **Select Java Options** dialog. Check the checkbox next to **Generate View Row Class** and click on **OK**.

This method will work on an individual record, so it goes into the view row class. Methods that work on the entire dataset of the view object should go into the view class.

Open your `RentalVORowImpl` class by clicking on the link in the **Java** tab. Scroll down to the bottom and add the following code:

```
    public String registerReturn () {
      Timestamp now = new Timestamp(System.currentTimeMillis());
      setReturnDate(now);
      return null;
    }
```

Then, navigate to **Build** | **Make RentalModel.jpr** to compile your code.

Adding Business Logic

Publishing your method

In order to make your new method available for other classes to call, you need to create a **Client Row Interface**. On the **Java** tab of the RentalVO view object, click on the pencil icon next to **Client Row Interface** as shown in the following screenshot:

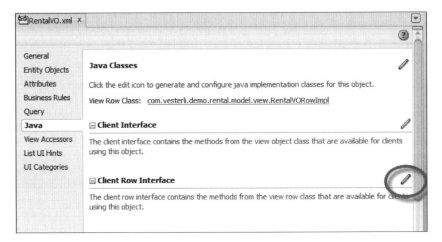

In the **Edit Client Row Interface** dialog, move your new registerReturn() method to the right-hand (**Selected**) box and click on **OK**. Your RentalVO view object should be updated to show some additional classes as shown in the following screenshot:

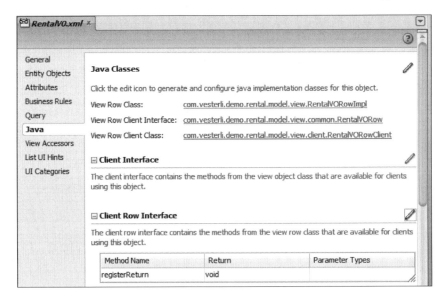

Establishing bindings

Like before, we want to perform a database commit when the user clicks on the button, so we need to create a binding for the `Commit` operation from our data control.

Because we have dropped items from the **Data Control** palette onto the `showRentals.jsff` page fragment, it already has a **Page Definition file**. Click on the **Bindings** tab to see it, and then use the green plus sign next to the **Bindings** heading to create an **action** binding for the `Commit` operation like we just did for the `rentDvd.jsff` page fragment in the preceding section.

Writing the bean code

Now all you need to do is to add business logic to the `returnDvd()` method in the `ReturnDvd` bean to find the current row and call the `registerReturn()` method on the view object. Use code like the following:

```
public String returnDvd() {
  // find selected row (the table iterator)
  RowKeySet sel = getFilmRentalTable().getSelectedRowKeys();
  Iterator selIter = sel.iterator();
  // get iterator for all data records
  BindingContainer bc =
    BindingContext.getCurrent().getCurrentBindingsEntry();
  DCBindingContainer dcb = (DCBindingContainer)bc;
  DCIteratorBinding rentalIter =
    dcb.findIteratorBinding("RentalUnreturnedIterator");
  RowSetIterator rsi = rentalIter.getRowSetIterator();
  // find the selected record in the data iterator
  Key key = (Key)((List)selIter.next()).get(0);
  RentalVORow r = (RentalVORow)rsi.getRow(key);
  r.registerReturn();
  OperationBinding ob = bc.getOperationBinding("Commit");
  ob.execute();
  return null;
}
```

> For the imports that exist in several packages, choose `BindingContainer` from `oracle.binding`, `BindingContext` from `oracle.adf.model`, `Key` from `oracle.jbo`, `List` from `java.util`, and `OperationBinding` from `oracle.binding`.

Adding Business Logic

The first part here uses the `getSelectedRowKeys()` method to get a `RowKeySet` and then gets an iterator to the selected rows. Because we chose option 3, there can only be one selected row, but the method always returns an iterator in order to allow for multiple selected rows.

The second part is the normal method for accessing data through a binding. In this case, we get a `RowSetIterator` from the data iterator, because this object has a `getRow(Key)` method that we can use to efficiently retrieve a single row by a `Key` object.

The `Key` line uses the `next()` method from the selection iterator to get all the data from the selected row, cast it to a `List`, and then get the first element. Because this is the key, it can be cast to a `Key` object that is then used to look up the `RentalVORow` object that represents the selected data record. In this object, we call the method to register a return, and the transaction is committed as before.

Marking items returned today

The last example of business logic coding in this chapter is showing the returned items in a different style (specifically, with a strikethrough line through the text). To do this, we will use **conditional formatting**.

> The appearance of elements in the application is controlled by the style properties. These can be hard-wired (for example, `color: Green;`), but they can also be set to dynamic values using Expression Language. You can refer to a bean value (for example, `#{pageFlowScope.myBean.colorAttribute}`) or to a value from the underlying data binding (for example, `#{row.bindings.TextFormat.inputValue}`).

Creating a transient attribute

In this case, we will create a new attribute in the `RentalVO` view object and write code in the `RentalVORowImpl` class to determine the value to return when the user interface requests it.

First, open the `RentalVO` view object and click on the **Attributes** subtab. Click on the green plus sign and choose **New Attribute**. This creates a new **transient** attribute, that is, one that is not based on the entity object and will not be stored in the database. Give it the name `TextFormat`. JDeveloper automatically adds accessors for this new attribute to the view row Java class.

Binding the new attribute

The new attribute is not automatically added to the bindings. Open the `showRentals.jsff` page fragment and switch to the **Bindings** tab. Click on the `RentalUnreturned` tree binding and then on the pencil icon next to the **Bindings** header.

Move the new `TextFormat` attribute from the **Available Attributes** box to the **Display Attributes** box as shown in the following screenshot:

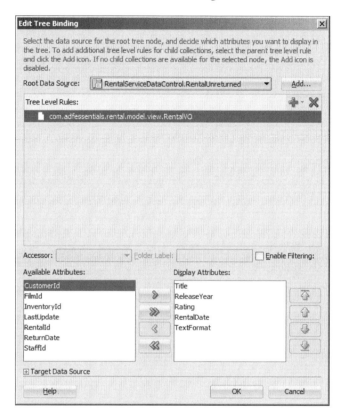

Coding the attribute return value

Find the `RentalVORowImpl.java` class in the **Application Navigator** (it's a sub-node under the `RentalVO` view object node in the Model project). If you scroll through this class, you will find that it has setter and getter methods for all attributes, including the new `TextFormat` attribute:

```
public String getTextFormat() {
  return (String) getAttributeInternal(TEXTFORMAT);
}
```

Adding Business Logic

```
/**
 * Sets <code>value</code> as the attribute value for
 * the calculated attribute TextFormat.
 * @param value value to set the  TextFormat
 */
public void setTextFormat(String value) {
  setAttributeInternal(TEXTFORMAT, value);
}
```

In this case, we want to override the getter, that is, replace the content of the method with our own business logic. More specifically, we want to return a specific text string with special styling information in case the film has been returned.

Add a new constant at the top of the class:

```
public class RentalVORowImpl extends ViewRowImpl
  implements RentalVORow {
  private static final String RETURNED_STYLING =
    "text-decoration:line-through;";
```

Also, change the getter method `getTextFormat()` to contain the following:

```
public String getTextFormat() {
  String retval = null;
  if(getReturnDate() != null) {
    retval = RETURNED_STYLING;
  }
  return retval;
}
```

This logic means that the row has a return date; the `getTextFormat()` method returns the text string `text-decoration:line-through;`. If there is no return date, the method returns `null`.

Using the attribute value

Finally, we need to use this bean value to change the appearance of the fields in the rental table.

Find `af:inputText` in the first column of the table on the `showRentals.jsff` page fragment and set the **ContentStyle** attribute to `#{row.bindings.TextFormat.inputValue}`.

> The reference to #{binding ...} works for individual attributes. When you need to work with the binding values for the current row of a multi-row component such as a table or a tree, you need to use #{row.binding ...}.

Repeat this process for the input text elements in the remaining columns. When you run the application, you will see that all fields in the row change to the strikeout look when you click on the **Return** button. The screenshot below shows the second rental has just been returned:

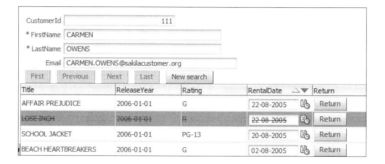

Other ideas

If you want to allow the user to cancel the return, you could create another button with the text Cancel return in the same column. You could also create a bean method to "un-return" the item by clearing the return date, and then use a bean method to control which of the two buttons would be rendered (using the **Rendered** property).

Summary

In this chapter, you have seen some examples of how to add Java code to your application to implement the specific business logic your application needs. There are many, many more places and ways to add logic -- as you work with ADF, you will continually come across new business requirements that force you to figure out how to add code to your application in new ways. Fortunately, there are other books, websites, online tutorials, and training that you can use to add to your ADF skillset -- refer to http://www.adfessentials.com for a starting point.

Until now, we have kept everything in one application workspace in JDeveloper. That's fine for small applications, but if you are building something larger than the little demo application in this book, you will need a way to split your application up into independent modules. That's the topic of *Chapter 5, Building Enterprise Applications*.

5
Building Enterprise Applications

So far, we have kept everything in one workspace for simplicity. If you are the only developer on the project, this approach works well. But in a larger setting with many developers, you need to set up a good structure to ensure that people do not get in each other's way.

 If you are developing ADF on your own as a one-man team, feel free to skip this chapter the first time you read the book (but do come back to it when you start on a larger project).

Whenever you start working on a development project, remember to decide on a project abbreviation of 3 to 5 characters that you can use in Java package names, filenames, and so on. For the DVD rental application used as an example in this book, we will use DRA.

Structuring your code

As you have seen in previous chapters, even a small application contains quite a few objects—entity objects, view objects, application modules, task flows, page fragments, managed beans, and many others. A large application will have hundreds or thousands of objects, so it becomes very important to keep everything in a logical structure. This allows you to divide work among the members of your team, and also ensures that everyone can find what they need.

Workspaces and projects

You've been working with only one workspace so far, but a larger application becomes unmanageable if you try to keep everything in one workspace.

> JDeveloper uses the word "application" for a workspace. This wording is imprecise, because only fairly-small applications will only use one workspace. Additionally, you will have many workspaces that are not complete applications. Whenever you see JDeveloper use the word "application", think "workspace".

Inside a workspace, you have one or more projects that can have dependencies on each other. We already saw dependencies in *Chapter 2, Creating Business Services*, where we defined a dependency on our `FameworkExtension` project. When you create an application of type **Fusion Web Application (ADF)**, JDeveloper creates two projects where the `View` project depends on the `Model` project. You can also have simple workspaces with only one project, or more advanced workspaces containing many projects.

With the help of ADF libraries, it is easy to use the output of a project in other workspaces. This allows a number of smaller development teams to work on separate subsystems so your large application is built in a modular fashion.

The workspace hierarchy

You should think of your workspaces as placed in a hierarchy (similar to object inheritance). Your basic, low-level workspaces can be included in higher-level subsystem workspaces, and the subsystem workspaces can be combined into the master application shown as follows:

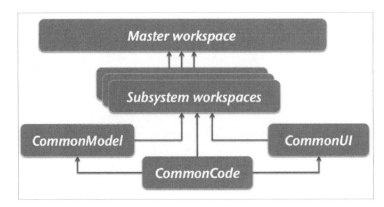

We have already built framework extension classes in *Chapter 2, Creating Business Services*. These should go into the **Common Code Workspace** together with all the other general utility classes you build during the course of the project.

In *Chapter 3, Creating Task Flows and Pages*, you built page flow templates and page templates before you built the actual pages. In a larger, real-life application, these should go into **Common UI Workspace**. If you decide to customize the way the application looks (using a technique known as "skinning"), the stylesheet and other elements of the skin also go into the Common UI Workspace.

Similar to the Common UI Workspace, you should have a **Common Model Workspace** for all your entity objects. You only need one entity object for each database table, so unless your application is very large, it makes sense to keep these together in one workspace. This workspace can also be used for View objects that are common to the entire application; for example, View objects used for value lists.

The **Subsystem Workspaces** are where you develop the actual screens that the user sees. Depending on your application and the size of your team, you can have many or few subsystem workspaces. A subsystem should contain a coherent subset of the total application—between three and ten workspaces are typical, but a large application can have dozens.

> If you are using task flows with page fragments, your task flows are not directly runnable. In this case, your subsystem should include one or more test pages to run your subsystem in isolation for debugging and testing.

All of your subsystem workspaces are combined into the **Master Workspace** that defines the full application. The Master Workspace is where common elements such as application-wide menus are defined, and application security is typically also added here.

The directory structure

Your entire application should be placed into a base folder with subfolders for each application workspace.

Additionally, you need to decide on a place to put the ADF libraries that have been released by the build/deployment manager. Typically, you create a directory inside the Master Application Workspace for released ADF libraries.

Using version control

Of courses, you need to use a version control system for your application. It would be nice if we could use a modern distributed versioning system such as GIT, but that is unfortunately not possible. At the time of writing, two different branches of the JDeveloper product exist:

- The 11gR1 branch (11.1.1.x version numbers) that supports GIT, but not ADF Essentials and GlassFish
- The 11gR2 branch (11.1.2.x version numbers) that support JSF 2.0, ADF Essentials, and GlassFish, but not GIT

Hopefully, by the time you read this, Oracle will have delivered the promised JDeveloper Version 12c, which supposedly will support both ADF Essentials/GlassFish and GIT version control.

Therefore, this book has to use Subversion to illustrate version control in enterprise ADF applications. The Subversion client is normally installed automatically in JDeveloper 11gR2—if it is not there, use **Help** | **Check for Updates** to find and install it. Before you can start using version control in JDeveloper, you must create a connection to a repository. This is done with the **Create Connection** command on the **Versioning** menu, where you need to provide a repository URL, a connection name, and username/password for the repository.

After creating the connection, you should change a setting in JDeveloper to make it automatically commit new files. Navigate to **Tools** | **Preferences** | **Versioning** | **Subversion**. You might have to click on **Load Extension** the first time you use the versioning features in JDeveloper. Then, choose **General** and make sure the checkbox **Automatically Add New Files on Committing Working Copy** is selected as shown in the following screenshot:

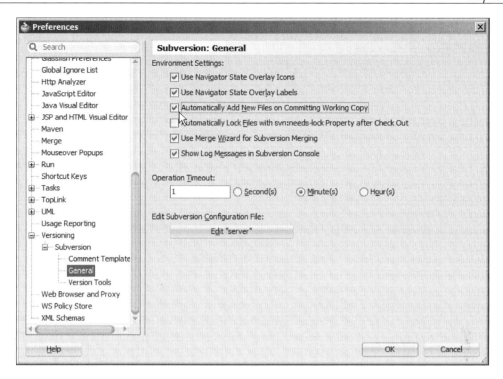

If you don't select this checkbox, you will manually have to monitor the **Pending Changes** panel (**Versioning**, **Pending Changes**) to add new files. Because a simple action in JDeveloper sometimes creates multiple files that you don't immediately see, it is a good idea to let JDeveloper automatically add new files as they are created.

As already mentioned, at least the build/deployment manager needs a version control client outside JDeveloper in order to handle ADF libraries. The examples in this book use TortoiseSVN, which integrates into the Windows Explorer.

>
> **Use the same Subversion client**
>
> If you are running JDeveloper 11.1.2.4, the built-in JDeveloper client is 1.7.x. In order for JDeveloper and TortoiseSVN to work together, also use a 1.7.x version of TortoiseSVN. The latest TortoiseSVN (1.8.x) will create Version 1.8 working directories that JDeveloper can't read.

Building Enterprise Applications

Working with ADF libraries

When we started with the DVD rental application in *Chapter 2, Creating Business Services*, we created a **Fusion Web Application (ADF)**. This creates a workspace with both a model and a view/controller project with the right technologies selected. In this chapter, you will see how we can also use a **Custom Application** workspace and select the relevant technologies ourselves.

Remember to use separate Java package names for each workspace, including subsystem workspaces. When you combine libraries from different workspaces, you only have the package name to find out where each component comes from. If you accidentally use the same package name twice, you might get subtle and hard-to-find bugs once you collect all your ADF libraries in the master application workspace.

ADF libraries are built from projects inside workspaces, so each workspace will produce one or more ADF libraries for other workspaces to use. An ADF library is in essence a regular `.jar` file, but with some added metadata to allow JDeveloper to recognize specific ADF constructs (task flows, business components) inside the file.

Version control outside JDeveloper

Because the ADF libraries you produce don't show up in the Application Navigator in JDeveloper, it is easiest to version control them outside JDeveloper. If you are using Subversion, TortoiseSVN is a good client that integrates with Windows Explorer for right-click version control.

Creating ADF libraries

In each workspace, you work until you have implemented some agreed functionality, tested and debugged it, and checked it into your version control system. Then, you create an ADF library that the build/deployment manager then releases for everybody else in the project to use.

To create an ADF library from a project, right-click on the project and choose **Deploy**, **New Deployment Profile**. Choose **ADF Library JAR File** and give your deployment profile a name. Use a naming standard such as `adflib<application abbreviation><library name>` for example, `adflibDraCommonCode`.

In the **Edit ADF Library JAR Deployment Profile Properties** dialog, always remember to choose **Connections** and change the setting for **Include** to **Connection Name Only** as shown in the following screenshot:

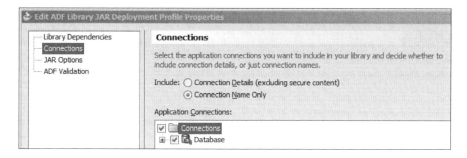

You do not want your library to include connection details—if your library contains specific connection information for connecting to your development database, the application will fail when moved to the test environment.

When you click on **OK**, your deployment profile is created. You can now right-click on the project again, click on **Deploy**, and choose your deployment profile. You might be prompted where to deploy to—in that case, just select **Deploy to ADF Library JAR File** and then click on **Finish**. This will create a `.jar` file with the same name as your deployment profile in the deploy subdirectory under your project.

> You can always edit your deployment profiles by right-clicking on the project and choosing **Project Properties** and then **Deployment**.

Because the ADF library file does not show up in JDeveloper, you need to go to the filesystem and check the ADF library `.jar` file into your source control system manually.

Releasing ADF libraries

Once the team responsible for a specific workspace has built an ADF library, it is the responsibility of a build/deployment manager to release it for use by the rest of the project. Depending on the level of formality in your project, this release procedure can take many forms. In an informal project, the build/deployment manager might simply talk to the developers to make sure that they have performed agreed tests. In a project with formal quality gates, the ADF library might be subjected to various tests before being released to the rest of the project.

Once the build/deployment manager is satisfied, he/she retrieves the ADF library file from the source control repository (in the workspace), copies it to the master ADF library location, and checks it in to the source control system.

Using ADF libraries

In order to add an ADF library to a project, you should create a filesystem connection to the directory containing your ADF library JAR files. To do this, open the **Resource Palette** from the **View** menu. Click on the **New** button in the **Resource Palette** and choose **New Connection | File System** as shown in the following screenshot:

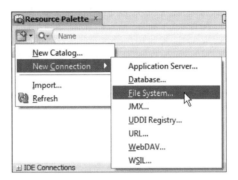

Give your connection a name and point to the location where you have decided to keep ADF libraries released by the build/deployment manager (for example, adfjars in your Master Application Workspace).

Now, the **Resource Palette** will show the available libraries in this directory. To actually use a library in a project, simply select the project in the **Application Navigator** and right-click on a library in the **Resource Palette** and choose **Add to Project**. You can also drag a library from the **Resource Palette** onto the project.

Example application

The rest of this chapter illustrates the preceding concepts by showing how to re-build the example DVD rental application in a proper enterprise application structure. Naturally, the descriptions are going to be somewhat less detailed—if you need the detailed instructions on how to build a specific part of the application, refer to the previous chapters. For brevity, this chapter will give explicit directions for package names, directories, and so on.

Conceptually, we are cutting the existing application up into five parts—in practice, we will be building five new application workspaces.

There are all kinds of complicated interdependencies in ADF projects. It is theoretically possible to make five copies of the existing application and delete various parts from each, but in practice, it will take more time to fix all the broken references than simply building everything again.

Creating the Master Application Workspace

As you saw earlier, we need a **Master Workspace** to collect the output of each subsystem workspace. For now, we will just create the workspace and the directory for ADF libraries—later in this chapter, we will add a master page and other elements to glue the various subsystems together in a complete application.

Creating the workspace

Create a new generic application workspace by selecting **File | New | General | Applications | Custom Application**. Call your application `DraMaster`, place it in the directory `C:\adfessentials\mywork\DraMaster`, and give it the name `com.adfessentials.dra`.

We are using DRA because we decided that this is the abbreviation for our DVD rental application.

The wizard asks you for the name of one project. Also call this project `DraMaster` and include the following from the **Project Features** list:

- ADF Business Components
- ADF Faces
- HTML and CSS
- ANT

Building Enterprise Applications

Some of these project features automatically include other features that they depend on. When you have added all the features, your screen should look like this:

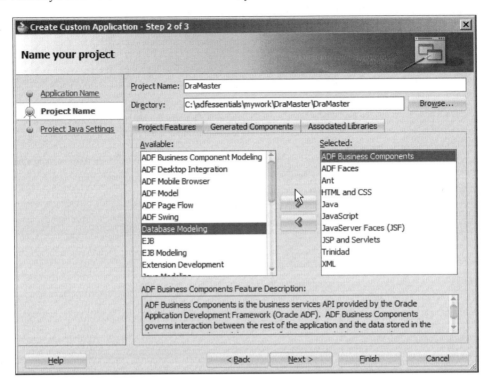

Just click on **Finish** to create your Master Application Workspace.

Adding to source control

To place the Master Application under version control, simply choose **Versioning, Version Application** and go through the **Import to Subversion** wizard (or similar if you are using a different version control system).

If you are using Subversion in a standard branches/tags/trunk layout, select the trunk node and click on the button at the top-right to create a new remote folder called `Master` as shown in the following screenshot:

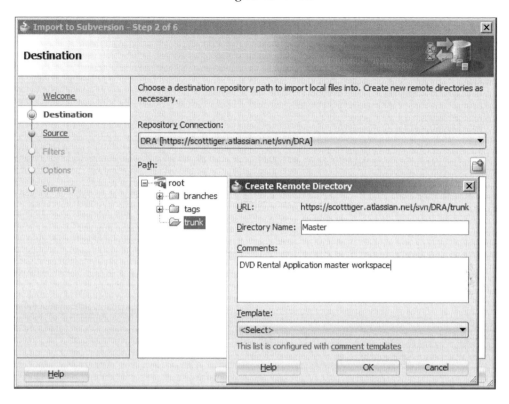

Make sure your newly created remote folder is selected before you click on **Next**. Then, go through the rest of the wizard to import your code.

 The idea is that each application workspace goes into its own folder under `trunk`.

Building Enterprise Applications

When the import completes, you should see a little extra icon at the bottomleft of each node in the Application Navigator and a Subversion version number after each element, as shown in the following screenshot:

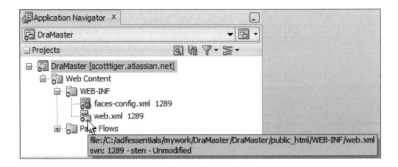

If you point to an element in the **Application Navigator**, you will be told its Subversion status (version, last user, unmodified/modified/new).

Creating the ADF library folder

Next, open a file explorer and change to the Master Workspace directory (`C:\adfessentials\mywork\DraMaster`). Create a new folder called `adfjars` here — this is the folder where the build/deployment manager will place all approved ADF libraries.

If you are using TortoiseSVN, this directory should show up with a question mark icon, indicating that it is not yet under source control. Right-click on the `adfjars` directory and choose **TortoiseSVN | Add** as shown in the following screenshot:

The icon on the folder changes to a plus sign, indicating that the folder is scheduled to be added to Subversion. Right-click on the folder again and choose **SVN Commit** to actually commit the new folder to the Subversion repository.

Creating the CommonCode workspace

The CommonCode workspace should contain the framework extension classes (you saw how to build these in *Chapter 2, Creating Business Services*) as well as any other utility classes that you develop for the application.

Creating the workspace

In JDeveloper, create a new application workspace of type **Custom Application**:

1. In step 1 of the wizard, give your workspace the name DraCommonCode. Place it in directory C:\adfessentials\mywork\DraCommonCode and give it an application package prefix com.adfessentials.dra.

2. In step 2, give the project the name CommonCode and include the **ADF Business Components** feature (change it from **Available** to **Selected**). **Java** is automatically added.

3. In step 3, set the **Default Package** to com.adfessentials.dra.common.

> Use your application abbreviation in application workspace names, because this allows you to find the application workspace folders among other projects in your JDeveloper work directory. You don't need the application abbreviation in project names, because these are only used inside project workspaces.

Recreating the framework extension classes

In the CommonCode project, create four framework extension classes like you saw in *Chapter 2, Creating Business Services*. Place all of them in the package com.adfessentials.adf.framework:

- An EntityImpl class extending oracle.jbo.server.EntityImpl
- A ViewObjectImpl class extending oracle.jbo.server.ViewObjectImpl
- A ViewRowImpl class extending oracle.jbo.server.ViewRowImpl

- An `ApplicationModuleImpl` class extending `oracle.jbo.server.ApplicationModuleImpl`
- For all of these, just choose **File** | **New** | **Java** | **Class**, give a class name, choose the class to extend, and deselect all the checkboxes in the **Create Java Class** dialog.

Check your JDeveloper preferences

Before you start building ADF Business Components, check your JDeveloper settings to make sure they match the framework extension classes you just built. Under **Tools** | **Preferences** | **ADF Business Components** | **Base Classes**, check that you have set the values matching the preceding package names, as shown in the following screenshot:

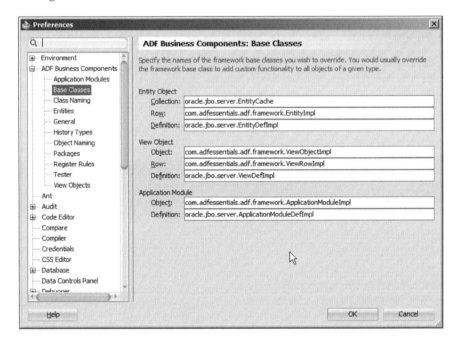

These settings control which base class JDeveloper uses when building ADF Business Components. We want JDeveloper to use the framework extension classes we have just created in the `CommonCode` project.

Adding to source control

Add this project to source control like you did for the Master Application (**Versioning** | **Version Application**). Remember to create a new remote folder under `trunk` called `CommonCode` and import the workspace into this folder.

Creating the ADF library

The final step is to create the ADF library. To do this, right-click on the `CommonCode` project and choose **Deploy | New Deployment Profile**. Choose **ADF Library JAR File** and deployment profile name `adflibDraCommonCode`.

> Use your application abbreviation in deployment profiles because these are used as ADF library filenames. It's nice to be able to tell directly from the name which project a given library belongs to.

When you have clicked on **OK** to create your deployment profile, right-click on the project again, click on **Deploy,** and choose your deployment profile. Choose **Deploy to ADF Library JAR File** and then click on **Finish**.

You can see the progress of the deployment in the log window:

```
[10:13:13 AM] ----   Deployment started.  ----
[10:13:13 AM] Target platform is Standard Java EE.
[10:13:13 AM] Running dependency analysis...
[10:13:13 AM] Building...
[10:13:14 AM] Deploying profile...
[10:13:15 AM] Wrote Archive Module to C:\adfessentials\mywork\
DraCommonCode\CommonCode\deploy\adflibDraCommonCode.jar
[10:13:15 AM] Elapsed time for deployment:  1 second
[10:13:15 AM] ----   Deployment finished.  ----
```

After first deployment, you get a shortcut on the context menu to deploy to a JAR file directly without going through the wizard. The deployment profile is stored in your `CommonCode` project file, so you need to commit your changes. On the **Versioning** menu, choose **Commit Working Copy**, provide an optional comment, and click on **OK**.

To check the ADF library into Subversion, open a file explorer and find the `deploy` directory inside the `CommonCode` project in the `DraCommonCode` workspace directory. Right-click on this directory and choose **TortoiseSVN | Add** as we did earlier for the `adfjars` directory. When you have added the directory, right-click on the `deploy` folder and choose **SVN Commit**. You can use any other Subversion client to achieve the same thing.

Releasing the ADF library

The developer's task is done when the ADF library is built and placed under version control, so now it's time for the build/deployment manager, whose tasks are:

1. Checking out the ADF library from the `CommonCode/deploy` directory.
2. Verifying it.
3. Copying it to the common `adfjars` directory in the `DraMaster` application workspace and committing it to version control.

> The amount of verification that the build/deployment manager does depends on your development style and the level of formality in your organization as mentioned previously.

For the example application, you are both developer and build/deployment manager. Simply copy the `adflibDraCommonCode.jar` file from `C:\adfessentials\mywork\DraCommonCode\CommonCode\deploy` to `C:\adfessentials\mywork\DraMaster\adfjars`. Then, right-click on the `.jar` file in the `adfjars` directory and choose **TortoiseSVN | Add** followed by **SVN Commit**.

Creating the CommonUI workspace

The CommonUI workspace must contain templates like the ones you created in *Chapter 3, Creating Task Flows and Pages*.

Creating the workspace

Create a new application workspace of type **Custom Application**:

1. In step 1 of the wizard, give your workspace the name `DraCommonUI`, directory `C:\adfessentials\mywork\DraCommonUI`, and application package prefix `com.adfessentials.dra`.
2. In step 2, give the project the name `CommonUI` and include the **ADF Faces** and **ADF Page Flow** features. Several other features are automatically added.
3. In step 3, set the **Default Package** to `com.adfessentials.dra.common.ui`.

Creating the templates

Create a task flow template like in *Chapter 3, Creating Task Flows and Pages*, by choosing **File | New | JSF/Facelets | ADF Task Flow Template**. Give it the name `dra-task-flow-template` and make sure **Create with Page Fragments** is checked.

Next, create a page fragment template by choosing **File | New | Web Tier | JSF/Facelets** and then **ADF Page Template**. Choose **Facelets** as document type and set **File Name** to DraPageFragmentTemplate.jsf.

> Items placed directly under public_html can be accessed directly from a web browser when the application runs, but items in the WEB-INF subdirectory cannot be accessed directly. That's why pages go into public_html, but templates and other elements that the users do not need to be able to access directly go into the WEB-INF subdirectory.

Add \WEB-INF to the end of the directory name as shown in the following screenshot:

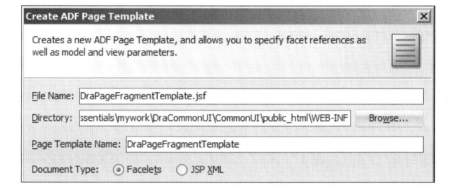

Choose **Use a Quick Start Layout** and leave the default selection of **One Column (Stretched)**. Define a facet with the name fragmentContent. When the template opens in the visual editor, drag a **Facet Definition** onto the center of the page template and select the fragmentContent facet name.

Finally, create a page template by choosing **File | New | Web Tier | JSF/Facelets** and then **ADF Page Template**. Choose **Facelets** as document type and give your page template the filename DraPageTemplate.jsf. Again, add \WEB-INF to the end of the directory. Choose **Use a Quick Start Layout** and select a one-column layout with a narrow, locked top box and a large stretchable box. Refer back to *Chapter 3, Creating Task Flows and Pages* for an illustration if needed. Define a facet with the name pageContent.

Building Enterprise Applications

When the template opens, drag a **Facet Definition** onto the center of the page template and select the facet name when prompted. Also, drag an **Output Text** component onto the top part of the page template and use the **Property Inspector** to set the value to DVD RENTAL App and set the style to **Green**, **x-large**, **bold**. Your JDeveloper window should look something like this:

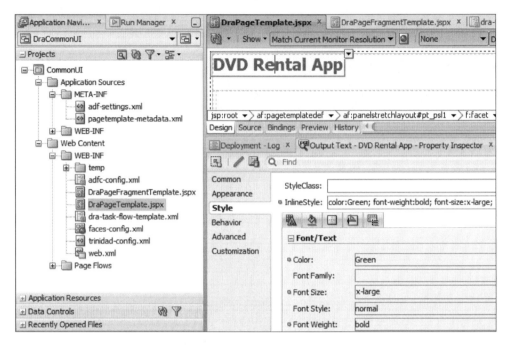

Your project should now contain the task flow template, the page fragment template, and the page template.

> 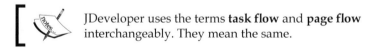 JDeveloper uses the terms **task flow** and **page flow** interchangeably. They mean the same.

Adding an ADF library

Your CommonUI workspace should include the output of the CommonCode workspace. We don't have anything in CommonCode right now that CommonUI needs, but later in the project we might add utility classes in CommonCode that we want to use in CommonUI.

To include the ADF library, we need to establish a **File System** connection as described earlier in the chapter:

1. Open the **Resource Palette** from the **View** menu.
2. Click on the **New** button in the **Resource Palette** and choose **New Connection, File System**.
3. Give your connection the name `DraLib` and point to the directory `C:\adfessentials\mywork\DraMaster\adfjars`.

Then, open the **File System** node in the **Resource Palette**, open your connection, and right-click on the `adflibDraCommonCode` library and choose **Add to Project** as shown in the following screenshot:

Adding to source control

Add this workspace to source control like you did for CommonCode (**Versioning | Version Application**). Remember to create a new remote folder under `trunk` called `CommonUI` and import the workspace into this folder.

> The ADF library (`adflibCommonCode.jar`) does not become part of the `CommonUI` project. Only the reference to it is stored.

Creating and releasing the ADF library

Finally, create an ADF library called `adflibDraCommonUI` following the same procedure as for `CommonCode` (new deployment profile and deploy).

Add the `deploy` folder to Subversion and commit. Copy the `adflibDraCommonUI.jar` file to `C:\adfessentials\mywork\DraMaster\adfjars`. Then, right-click on the `.jar` file in the `adfjars` directory and choose **TortoiseSVN | Add** followed by **SVN Commit**.

Creating the CommonModel workspace

The `CommonModel` workspace contains the Business Components that are common to the whole application. This is typically the entity objects and any common view objects used for lists of values across the application. In our simple example application, the CommonModel workspace will contain only entity objects.

Creating the workspace

Create a new application workspace of type **Custom Application**:

1. In step 1 of the wizard, give your workspace the name `DraCommonModel` and the application package prefix `com.adfessentials.dra`.
2. In step 2, give the project the name `CommonModel` and include the **ADF Business Components** feature. **Java** is automatically added.
3. In step 3, set the **Default Package** to `com.adfessentials.dra.common.model`.

Adding an ADF library

Your CommonModel workspace needs the framework extension classes in the CommonCode workspace, so you need to find the `adflibDraCommonCode` library in the **Resource Palette** and add it to your project. This allows the ADF Business Components in CommonCode to make use of the framework extension classes that have been packaged into that library.

Creating the entity objects

Create the four entity objects we need with the **Business Components from Tables** wizard (**File | New | Business Tier | ADF Business Components | Business Components from Tables**).

You first have to create a connection. Click on the green plus in the **Initialize Business Components Project** dialog and set up a MySQL connection to the `Sakila` database as we've done before. Use the connection name `Sakila` (port is 3306). Choose **SQL92** as the **SQL Platform** and chose **Java** as **Data Type Map**.

In step 1 of the wizard, click on **Query** and select the `customer`, `film`, `inventory`, and `rental` tables. Then, simply click on **Finish** to create the entity objects.

Like we did in *Chapter 2, Creating Business Services*, we need to change some of the default datatypes to avoid the complexity of working with custom domains. This is done on the **Attributes** subtab in the entity objects by right-clicking on the attribute and choosing **Change Type** as shown in the following screenshot:

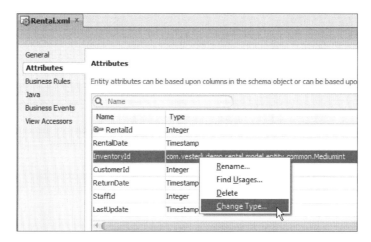

- In the `Rental` entity object, change the type for `InventoryId` to `Integer`
- In the `Rilm` entity object, change the type for the `Description` attribute to `String`
- In the `Film` entity object, change the type for the `ReleaseYear` attribute to `Integer`
- In the `Film` entity object, change the type for the `Rating` attribute to `String`
- In the `Film` entity object, delete the `SpecialFeatures` column

You might remember from *Chapter 2, Creating Business Services* that we did various clean-up tasks (fixing associations and so on). For the sake of brevity, we'll skip these here.

Adding to source control and creating the ADF library

This procedure is like before:

1. Add the workspace to version control from within JDeveloper (create a new remote folder called `CommonModel` in Subversion).

2. Create an ADF library deployment profile called `adflibDraCommonModel`. Remember to change the **Connections** setting to **Connection Name Only**. Then, deploy to an ADF library JAR file.
3. If needed, add the `deploy` folder to Subversion and commit. Then, copy the `adflibDraCommonModel.jar` file to `DraMaster\adfjars`, add it to Subversion, and commit.

Creating the RentDvd subsystem workspace

Each subsystem will contain a number of bounded task flows with their associated page fragments and managed beans as well as the underlying data structures in the form of **View** objects.

For the RentDvd subsystem, this is:

- The rental flow
- One page fragment
- One managed bean
- One **View** object

All subsystems have dependencies on CommonCode, CommonModel, and CommonUI, so they need to import these ADF libraries.

Creating the workspace

Create a new application workspace of type **Fusion Web Application (ADF)**:

1. In step 1 of the wizard, give your workspace the name `DraRentDvd` and the application package prefix `com.adfessentials.dra.rentdvd`.
2. In step 2, give your model project the name `RentDvdModel`.
3. In step 3, verify that the **Default Package** for the model is `com.adfessentials.dra.rentdvd.model`.
4. In step 4, give your view/controller project the name `RentDvdView`.
5. In step 5, verify that the **Default Package** for the model is `com.adfessentials.dra.rentdvd.view`.

Adding ADF libraries

Choose the `RentDvdModel` project and from the **Resource Palette**, add the libraries `adflibDraCommonCode` and `adflibDraCommonModel`.

Then, choose the `RentDvdView` project and add the libraries `adflibDraCommonCode` and `adflibDraCommonUI`.

We are only adding references to the libraries, so even though we refer to `adflibCommonCode` several times in this subsystem (and will do so in other subsystems as well), there will only be one instance of the ADF library in the finished application.

> If any of these libraries don't show up in the **Resource Palette**, right-click on the name of your **File System** connection and choose **Refresh** from the context menu. If any are still missing, you probably forgot to copy them from the `deploy` directory of the subsystem into the `adfjars` directory of the `DraMaster` application workspace.

Creating the view object

As you saw in *Chapter 3, Creating Task Flows and Pages*, the RentDvd page doesn't actually present any data—it only creates new records programmatically through the RentalBean. However, you still need a **View** object in order to allow the bean to create records.

Because you have attached the CommonModel ADF library (that contains a database connection name), your application already contains a database connection. You can see this in the **Application Navigator** under **Application Resources**. However, the connection might be marked with a small x as shown in the following screenshot:

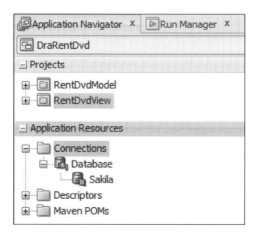

Building Enterprise Applications

This indicates that there is something you need to fix. Because you chose in the deployment profile to deploy the connection name only, some connection details are missing. In order to work with the `Sakila` connection in this workspace, you need to right-click on the connection and choose **Properties**. Provide the correct parameters (**Connection Type MySQL**, username/password, port `3306`, database name `sakila`).

Then, select the `RentDvdModel` project and choose **File | New | Business Tier | ADF Business Components | View Object**. Because this Model project has not been used before, the **SQL Platform** and **Data Type Map** are not set yet. As elsewhere, choose **SQL92** and **Java**.

In the **Create View Object** wizard, give your view object the name `RentalVO`. In step 2 of the wizard, you should see the entity object from your CommonModel workspace in the **Available** box. Double-click on the `Rental` entity object to move it to the **Selected** box as shown in the following screenshot:

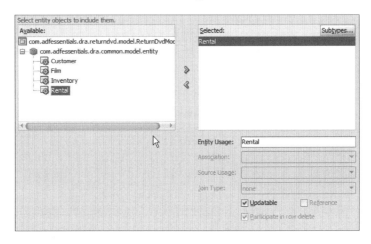

In step 3, select all the attributes. Then, simply click on **Finish** to create the view object.

Creating the application module

You also need an application module to contain an instance of this view object. Still in the `RentDvdModel` project, choose **File | New | Business Tier | ADF Business Components | Application Module**.

Give your application module the name `RentDvdService` and click on **Next**. In step 2 of the wizard, select the `RentalVO` view object to the right, correct the content of the **New View Instance** field to `RentalVO` (it defaults to something like `RentalVO1`), and click on the **>** button to move it to the right.

> The view object instances inside application modules by default get a number added to their name because each view object can be included several times in the application module (for example, with different view criteria).

You can now just click on **Finish** to close the wizard and create the application module.

Creating the task flow and page fragment

To create the task flow, select your **RentDvdView** project and choose **File | New | JSF/Facelets | ADF Task Flow**. Give it the name `rent-dvd-flow` and base it on the `dra-task-flow-template`. Drag a view activity onto the task flow from the **Component Palette** and give it the name `rentDvd`.

Double-click on the `rentDvd` activity to create the page fragment, choosing **Facelets** and `DraPageFragmentTemplate`. On this page, first add a `PanelFormLayout`, then add two fields to the panel form layout and set the labels to `Customer ID` and `Inventory ID`. Finally, add a button to the footer facet of the panel form layout and set the label to `Register rental`.

Adding a binding

Because we have not dropped anything on the page from the **Data Controls** palette, JDeveloper has not created the page binding file yet. To create this, right-click on the page and choose **Go to Page Definition** and say yes to create the file.

On this page, click on the green plus in the **Executables** box and choose an **iterator** binding. Select the `RentalVO` view object instance as shown in the following screenshot:

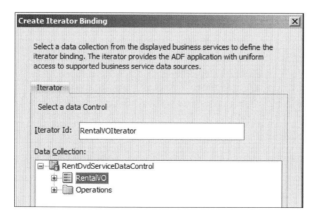

Building Enterprise Applications

The bean logic will be referring to this iterator name.

Adding the business logic

You already saw how to implement the business logic in *Chapter 4, Adding Business Logic*. The procedure involves:

- Creating a managed bean
- Creating properties in this bean with setters and getters and connecting these with the items on the screen
- Connecting the button with a method that creates a new `Rental` record

Refer back to *Chapter 4, Adding Business Logic* for the details.

Remaining work

1. Add the application workspace to version control from within JDeveloper (create a new remote folder called `RentDvd` in Subversion).
2. Create an ADF library deployment profile called `adflibDraRentDvd` in the `RentDvdView` project. Remember to change the **Connections** setting to **Connection Name Only**. Then, deploy to an ADF library JAR file.

> You only need to create an ADF library from the view project in a subsystem workspace. When you create a **Fusion Web Application (ADF)** workspace, JDeveloper automatically adds the necessary dependency so the `View` project will include the content of the `Model` project.

3. Add the `deploy` folder to Subversion and commit. Copy the `adflibDraRentDvd.jar` file to `DraMaster\adfjars` and then also add it to Subversion and commit.

If you want to test your subsystem, you will have to create a test page and drop the `rent-dvd-flow` onto this page as a static region like we did in *Chapter 3, Creating Task Flows and Pages*.

Creating the ReturnDvd subsystem workspace

The ReturnDvd subsystem will contain the return flow with its two page fragments. The procedure for building this in an enterprise setting is very similar to the way we just built the RentDvd subsystem.

Creating the workspace

Create a new application workspace of type **Fusion Web Application (ADF)**:

1. In step 1 of the wizard, give your workspace the name DraReturnDvd and the application package com.adfessentials.dra.returndvd.
2. In step 2, give your model project the name ReturnDvdModel.
3. In step 3, verify that the **Default Package** for the model is com.adfessentials.dra.returndvd.model.
4. In step 4, give your view/controller project the name ReturnDvdView.
5. In step 5, verify that the **Default Package** for the model is com.adfessentials.dra.returndvd.view.

Adding ADF libraries

Choose the ReturnDvdModel project, and from the **Resource Palette**, add the libraries adflibDraCommonCode and adflibDraCommonModel.

Then, choose the ReturnDvdView project and add the libraries adflibDraCommonCode and adflibDraCommonUI.

Creating the Customer view object

Like you did for the RentDvd subsystem, start by right-clicking on the Sakila database connection (under **Application Resources**), choose **Properties**, and provide the right values (**Connection Type MySQL**, username/password, port 3306, database name sakila).

Then, select the ReturnDvdModel project and choose **File | New, Business Tier | ADF Business Components | View Object**. Choose **SQL Platform: SQL92** and **Data Type Map: Java**.

In the **Create View Object** wizard, give your view object the name CustomerVO. In step 2 of the wizard, select the customer entity object. In step 3, shuttle the attributes FirstName, LastName, and Email to the **Selected** box. In step 4, you don't need to change anything. In step 5, fill in the **Order By** field with last_name, first_name and click on **Finish** to create the view object.

Also, add a **view criterion** to limit the view object to show only the customers that match the search criteria in the first screen as described in *Chapter 2, Creating Business Services*.

Building Enterprise Applications

Creating the Rental view object

To create the Rental view object, you need data from several entity objects. First, select your model project and then **File | New | Business Tier | ADF Business Components | View Object**.

In step 1 of the wizard, give your view object the name `RentalVO`.

In step 2, open the `.entity` node to the left and first shuttle the `Rental` entity object to the right-hand box. Then, select the `Inventory` entity object and shuttle it to the right. Check the association—it should be the one that contains "Inventory" and "Rental" in the name; for example, `FkRentalInventoryAssoc3.Inventory1`. Your screen should look like this:

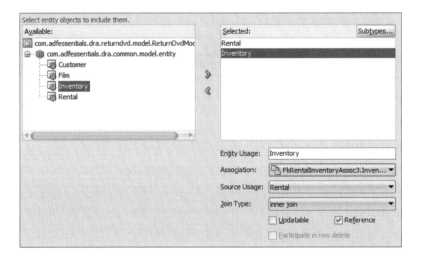

Then, shuttle the `Film` entity object to the right and select the association that contains "Inventory" and "Film" in the name; for example, `FkInventoryFilmAssoc3.Film2`.

> We have to choose associations because the Business Components from the Tables wizard build too many. In *Chapter 2, Creating Business Services*, we saw a correct cleanup of these superfluous associations.

In step 3, shuttle the `Title`, `ReleaseYear`, and `Rating` attributes from the `Film` entity object to the right as well as `RentalDate`, `ReturnDate`, and `CustomerId` from the `Rental` entity object.

Just click on **Next** to skip step 4, and in step 5, fill in the **Order By** with `rental_date`. Then, click on **Finish** to create the view object.

Finally, add a view criterion to limit the Rental view object to show only unreturned items. On the **Query** tab, add a new view criterion as above. Call it `UnreturnedCriteria` and add a line for attribute `ReturnDate` with operator **Is blank**.

Creating a View Link

The two view objects must be connected via a View Link. To create this, select the `Model` project and choose **File** | **New** | **Business Tier** | **ADF Business Components** | **View Link**. In step 1 of the **Create View Link** wizard, give the view link the name `CustomerRentalLink`. In step 2, set **Cardinality** to **0.1 to ***, expand the `CustomerVO` view object node on the left, and select the `CustomerId` attribute. On the right, expand the `RentalVO` view object node and also select the `CustomerId` attribute. Then, click on **Add** to add an attribute to the link. Your screen should look like this:

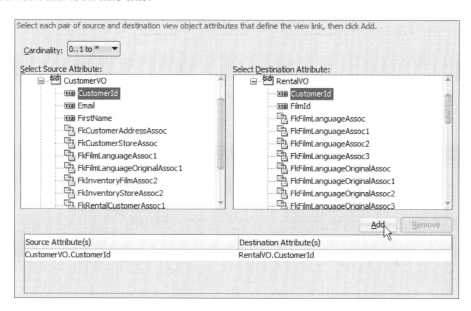

Then, click on **Next** and then on **Finish**.

Creating an application module

You need to place instances of these two view objects in an application module in order for the user interface to access them. Choose **File** | **New** | **Business Tier** | **ADF Business Components** | **Application Module** to start the **Create Application Module** wizard.

Building Enterprise Applications

In step 1 of the wizard, give the application module the name `ReturnDvdService`.

In step 2, expand the tree to see the two view objects.

First, select the `CustomerVO` view object and fill the **New View Instance** field with the value `CustomerSearchResult`. Then, click on the **>** button to create a view object instance in the right-hand box.

Next, select the node `RentalVO via CustomerRentalLink`, fill the **New View Instance** field with the value `RentalUnreturned`, and click on **>**.

Finally, select the `RentalVO` view object that is not indented under `CustomerVO`, fill in **New View Instance** with `RentalVO`, and click on**>**. Your screen should now look like this:

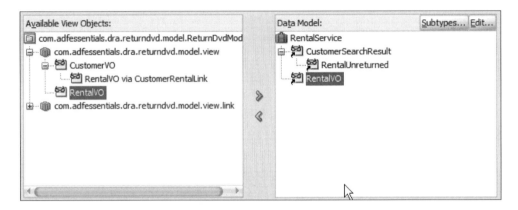

Click on the `CustomerSearchResult` view object instance and click on the **Edit** button and move the view criteria from the **Available** to the **Selected** box to apply the view criteria to this view object instance in the application module.

> View criteria applied to view object instances in an application module will always be applied. If you want to use the view criteria sometimes but not always, you can programmatically apply and remove it like you saw in one of the code examples in *Chapter 4 , Adding Business Logic*

Similarly, edit the `RentalUnreturned` view object instance and select the `UnreturnedCriteria`. Then, click on **Finish** to create the application module.

> If you have problems getting the naming and/or view criteria right, just create the application module. Afterwards, you can open it and use the **Data Model** tab to change view object instance names and view criteria.

Creating the task flow

In *Chapter 3, Creating Task Flows and Pages*, we built the return DVD task flow with two views (page fragments) and one method call. When finished, it should look like this:

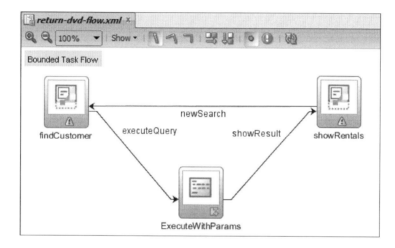

Refer back to *Chapter 3, Creating Task Flows and Pages* for the details. Remember to provide parameter values from `PageFlowScope` variables when adding the `ExecuteWithParams` method call.

Creating the Customer Search Page Fragment

To build the customer search screen, double-click on the `findCustomer` view in the `return-dvd-flow` task flow. Make sure `DraPageFragmentTemplate` is selected and click on **OK**.

Choose a **Panel Form Layout** from the **Component Palette** and place four **Input Text** components inside it. Use the **Property Palette** to provide labels and set the `Value` property to the correct variable: `#{pageFlowScope.searchCustomerId}`, `#{pageFlowScope.searchEmail}`, `#{pageFlowScope.searchFirstName}`, or `#{pageFlowScope.searchLastName}` (remember, the names are from when we dropped the `ExecuteWithParams` element onto the task flow).

Then, drop a **Button** component onto the footer facet of the panel form layout. Use the **Property Inspector** to set the button **Text** property to `Customer lookup` and choose `executeQuery` as the **Action**.

Creating the Rentals Page Fragment

Now double-click on the `showRentals` view in the task flow to create the page to show the customer and his or her rentals page.

First, add a **Panel Group Layout**, setting the **Layout** property to **Vertical**. Also, set the **StyleClass** property to `AFStretchWidth`.

Then, open the **Data Controls** panel in the **Application Navigator** and expand the `RentDvdServiceDataControl` node to see `CustomerSearchResult`. Drag the `CustomerSearchResult` element onto the page fragment and drop it as an **ADF Form**. In the **Edit Form Fields** dialog, check the **Include Navigation Controls** checkbox and click on **OK**.

Finally, expand the `CustomerSearchResult` node in the **Data Controls** panel and drag the `RentalUnreturned` element onto the page below the buttons. In the **Create** popup menu, choose **Table | ADF Table**. In the **Edit Table Columns** dialog, remove the `FilmId`, `RentalId`, and `ReturnDate` columns. Check the checkbox **Enable Sorting** and click on **OK**.

To fix the layout to use all available space, you need to select the `af:table` component in the **Structure** panel. In the **Property Inspector,** set the **StyleClass** property to `AFStretchWidth` in order to make the table fill all available space. Then, select the `af:table` element, find the **Id** of the `Title` column (typically something like `c1`), and set the **ColumnStretching** property of the table to the value corresponding to the title column (`column:c1`). This makes the table allocate any extra space on the screen to this column.

Registering a return

You can add a button and business logic to register the return of a rented DVD in the same way as you saw in *Chapter 4 , Adding Business Logic*.

Remaining work

Carry out the following steps:

1. Add the application workspace to version control from within JDeveloper (create a new remote folder called `ReturnDvd` in Subversion).

2. Create an ADF library deployment profile called `DraReturnDvd` in the `ReturnDvdView` project. Remember to change the **Connections** setting to **Connection Name Only**. Then, deploy to an ADF library JAR file.

3. Add the `deploy` folder to Subversion and commit. Copy the `adflibDraReturnDvd.jar` file to `DraMaster\adfjars` and then also add it to Subversion and commit.

Again, if you want to test your subsystem, you will have to create a test page and drop the `return-dvd-flow` task flow onto this page as a static region like before.

Finishing the Master Application Workspace

We've taken the RentalApp application apart. It has been split into five subsystems that have each been deployed as their own ADF Library and we have copied these to the `adfjars` directory in the master application. Now it's time to put the application back together.

The master application will contain the two task flows from the RentDvd and ReturnDvd subsystems and a master application page. In this example, we will simply place the two task flows on separate tabs on a master page, but in a real-life enterprise application, you will often use a menu and a dynamic region to change between task flows.

Adding the ADF libraries

The `DraMaster` workspace needs all five ADF Libraries—simply add them to the project from the **Resource Palette**.

Fix the `Sakila` database connection as you saw earlier in the chapter.

 Because you deploy only connection names to your ADF libraries, the user of the libraries must define the `Sakila` connection details.

Create the master page

An ADF enterprise application will contain many bounded task flows, each containing many page fragments—but it will have few pages, possibly only one. You need one page for every direct access point your application needs—if you want three different entry points to the application with three different URLs, you need three pages.

In the DVD rental application in this book, we will have one page with two tabs for the two taskflows. Create a page with the name `DvdRental` and choose to base it on the `rentalPageTemplate`. Set the **Title** property of the `af:document` element to `DVD Rental Application`.

Drop a **Panel Tabbed** component onto the `content` facet of the page. This component automatically adds the first tab, which is `af:showDetailItem`. Set the **Text** property for the tab to `Rental` and drop the `rent-dvd-flow` (from the `adflibDraRentDvd` on the **Resource Palette**) on the tab as a static region.

Drop another `ShowDetailItem` onto the `af:panelTabbed` component and set the **Text** property to `Return`. Drop the `return-dvd-flow` from `adflibDraReturnDvd` onto the new tab as a static region.

Your master application is now ready to run. Either run it in the built-in WebLogic server or deploy it to your GlassFish server to test it out.

Summary

In this chapter, we have re-built the application that we developed in the last three chapters, but this time in a proper, scalable structure using separate workspaces for separate parts of the application. Based on ADF libraries built on the three foundation workspaces, we have developed two separate subsystems and deployed these as ADF libraries as well.

Finally, we built a master application putting these libraries together to a finished application. In this way, you can build any size of system by splitting it up in various task flows and subsystems.

If you followed along in JDeveloper while reading this chapter, you will probably have experienced a thing or two that did not work the first time. To find errors, logging and debugging is an important part of application development. That is the topic of *Chapter 6, Debugging ADF Applications*.

6
Debugging ADF Applications

Naturally, your applications work the first time. But in case you want to help your friends and colleagues, who do not write code as flawlessly as you, this chapter describes how to find out what their application is doing using the ADF logging features and the JDeveloper debugging support.

ADF logging

Beginner programmers tend to litter their code with `System.out.println()` calls because that's the `print` statement used in the ubiquitous "Hello World" examples. As programmers gain experience, they tire of having to remove all of these statements before putting code into production and start using a proper logging framework.

There are several options for logging in Java — some of the most well-known are `log4j` and `Logback`. However, in an ADF application, it is recommended to use the `ADFLogger`.

> The `ADFLogger` can write its log output in **Oracle Diagnostics Logging** (**ODL**) format that can be read and analyzed by both the developer (in JDeveloper) and by a WebLogic administrator (using Oracle Enterprise Manager Grid Control). If you are running your application in GlassFish, your operations people do not have grid control. However, since `ADFLogger` offers all necessary logging functionality, it makes sense to use this logging framework just in case your application will some day be deployed to a WebLogic server.

Creating a logger

In every code element in your application, you create an instance of the `ADFLogger` class with the `ADFLogger.createADFLogger()` method. This method takes a class as a parameter—you will normally pass it the class that you are placing the logger inside:

```
package com.vesterli.demo.adf.xx.view.beans;

public TestBean {
  private final ADFLogger logger =
      ADFLogger.createADFLogger(TestBean.class);

  public void TestBean() {
  }
}
```

By passing in the class itself, you build a hierarchy of loggers, each with the same name as the class. This allows you to control the logging level for individual classes so you can log with great detail in the classes you are interested in and set a less detailed logging level for other classes.

Adding log statements

The actual logging is done by calling methods on the `ADFLogger` object like this:

```
public void MyMethod() {
  //do stuff
  logger.fine("Just did stuff");
  try {
    // do risky stuff
    logger.finer("Doing risky stuff");
  } catch (Exception e) {
    logger.warning("Something went wrong");
    logger.warning(e);
  }
}
```

You select a log level when you write your log statements. The available levels (in decreasing order of severity) are:

- SEVERE
- WARNING
- INFO
- CONFIG

[192]

- FINE
- FINER
- FINEST

In every project, your developer guidelines should define how you decide to use the logging levels to ensure uniform usage throughout the code.

> Write a simple set of developer guidelines, even if you are the only developer working on the application. It will be useful if somebody else takes over the application later. It will also be useful if you have to go back to the application yourself after several years.

An example of some logging guidelines is illustrated in the following table:

Log level	Usage
SEVERE	Critical errors that prevent the application from continuing. Set up monitoring of your logfiles so that the operational staff are informed if this kind of error shows up in the logs.
WARNING	Warnings that indicate misconfigurations, missing data, or failures from other components or external systems. Use these in catch clauses for errors you do not expect; for example, SQLException. Exceptions that are expected and handled (for example, if InvalidNumberException can be handled by substituting a zero value) should not produce WARNING logs.
INFO	Application logging intended for business users.
CONFIG	Information about configurations read from property files, databases, or other sources. Information about initialization of classes.
FINE	Information about method calls. Normally used only once or twice in a method when entering (showing parameters received) and/or leaving (showing the return value).
FINER	More detailed logging. This is allowed several times in a method.
FINEST	Most detailed log level. Logging inside loops should be this level.

Business logging

When designing the log messages, keep in mind who you are writing for. Most developers write only for other developers, but your application should also log information for business users:

- Messages for developers can refer to internal variable values and can be very technical. These messages will often refer to system-generated ID values that make sense to a developer looking something up in the database.
- Messages to business users should use terms they recognize and the values actually displayed in the user interface. Do not show internal system-generated keys to business users—instead, use values that a user can use to look up data within the application.

Developer messages might look like this:

```
ProcessInvoice() called: InvoiceId=8765123, firstInvoice=true
InvoiceLines.count=0, break
```

A business message would look more like this:

```
Started processing invoice 667788
Processing aborted, no invoice lines
```

If you reserve one log level (for example, INFO) for business messages, you can allow application "super users" to see the logfiles in case they want to investigate how a specific business item was processed by the system.

JDeveloper shortcuts

Since you will be (or should be) writing a lot of log statements in your code, it makes sense to use the JDeveloper **code template** feature to create shortcuts for creating and using loggers.

To add a code template, navigate to **Tools | Preferences | Code Editor | Code Templates**. The **Code Templates** dialog appears as shown in the following screenshot:

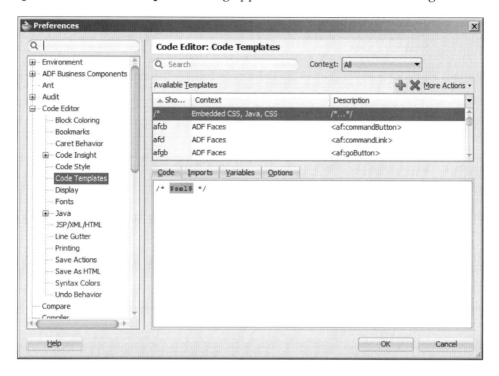

Click on the green plus icon to add a new template. To create a template for adding a logger, define **Shortcut** as `aldef`, set **Context** to **Java Type Members**, and fill in **Description** with something like `Create a new ADF logger`.

Fill in the tabs as follows:

1. On the **Code** tab, write `private final ADFLogger logger = ADFLogger.createADFLogger($classname$.class);`.
2. On the **Imports** tab, write `oracle.adf.share.logging.ADFLogger`.

Debugging ADF Applications

3. On the **Variables** tab, you will see a `classname` variable (because you used it on the **Code** tab). Set the **Type** value for this to `Class Name` and remove the checkmark in the **Editable** column. Your screen should look like this:

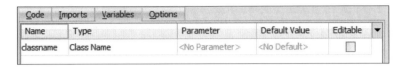

Now place the cursor at the top of your class definition, write `aldef`, and press *Ctrl + Enter*. JDeveloper will add the content of the **Code** tab for this code template at the cursor and add the content of the **Imports** tab at the top of the class with the other inserts.

Use the same dialog box to add shortcuts for the logging statements you need. For example, to log at the `FINEST` level, you could add a logger with shortcut `alf3` and the code `logger.finest("$log$");`. In this case, the default variable handling (to place the cursor at the variable) is OK, so you do not need to change anything on the **Variables** tab. Your code template screen should look like this:

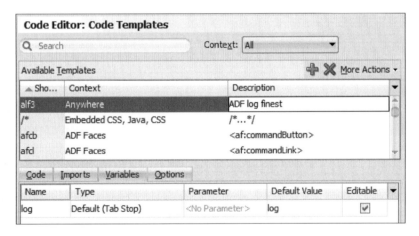

When you need a log statement of level `FINEST`, you can now place the cursor where you want the statement, write `alf3`, and press *Ctrl + Enter*. JDeveloper adds the log statement from the **Code** tab and places the cursor at the variable definition (between the quotes) so you can write your log statement.

> Oracle Product Manager Duncan Mills has created a comprehensive set of logging shortcuts that you can download and install.
> See http://blogs.oracle.com/groundside/entry/adventures_in_adf_logging_part1.

Reading the logs

As your application runs in the built-in WebLogic server, you will see the log output in the **Log** window (by default at the bottom of the JDeveloper window).

ADF logging is controlled by the `logging.xml` file. JDeveloper offers a nice interface for managing this file for the built-in WebLogic server. You can access this from the **Log** window by clicking on **Actions** (in the top-right corner of the log window) and choosing **Configure Oracle Diagnostic Logging** as shown in the following screenshot:

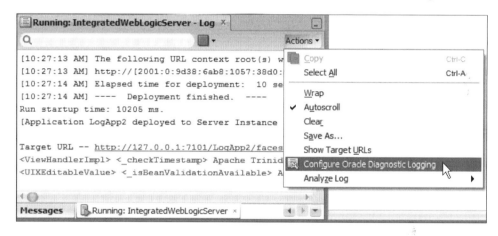

Note that this menu item only appears when the built-in WebLogic server is running.

Debugging ADF Applications

The `logging.xml` file opens in a dedicated log level editor that allows you to navigate the hierarchy of loggers and set their levels as shown in the following screenshot:

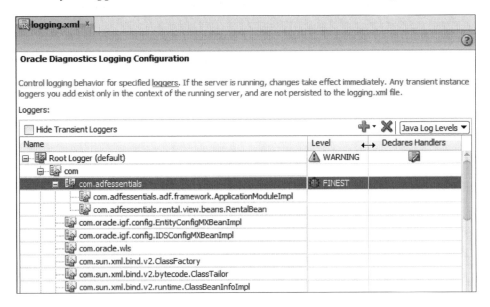

There are two types of loggers:

- **Transient loggers** are created when a class is instantiated and disappear again when the class is no longer used
- **Persistent loggers** are explicitly defined and permanent

You should create a persistent logger for your application with a logger name that corresponds to the Java package root of your application. So, if your company base package is `com.company` and your application abbreviation is `dra`, create a base logger called `com.company.dra`. This will control the logging for all classes in your application.

You can define more specific loggers as needed; for instance, for individual subsystems. Because of the hierarchy, you can have your `com.company.dra` logger set to `INFO` and have a subpackage, `com.company.dra.rentdvd`, set to `FINE` to see more detailed logging from this subsystem.

>
> **Logging SQL statements**
> If you want to see the SQL statements that ADF is sending to your database, create a new persistent logger for `oracle.jbo` and set it to `FINEST`. This will produce a lot of logging, and among it will be the actual SQL statements and bind variable values. Search the log for `BaseSQLBuilderImpl` to see all the SQL your application uses.

Logging in GlassFish

When you deploy your application to GlassFish, your log statements are written to the `server.log` file. You can view this file from the GlassFish admin web page (by default running on port `4848`) by navigating to **Server | View Log Files**, or you can just look at the file itself—it's found under your domain, for example, `C:\adfessentials\glassfish3\glassfish\domains\domain1\logs\server.log`.

>
> The log lines are rather long—if you want a different format, you can create your own formatter class as described by user Kawo on the site Stack Overflow:
>
> `http://stackoverflow.com/questions/9609380/glassfish-3-how-do-you-change-the-default-logging-format`
>
> You can also redirect your log output to a `syslog` service as described by Markus Eisele on his blog:
>
> `http://blog.eisele.net/2012/07/glassfish-operations-log-notifications.html`

GlassFish logging can be controlled by changing the `logging.properties` file in the `config` directory in your domain, for example, `C:\adfessentials\glassfish3\glassfish\domains\domain1\config\logging.properties`. This file contains three sections:

- A general header (all comment)
- Properties that apply to the whole domain
- Settings for individual loggers

Controlling domain logging

In the section on the domain, you will find general settings that apply to all logging in the domain. Some values you might want to change are:

- `com.sun.enterprise.server.logging.GFFileHandler.file` allows you to change the logfile location and name
- `com.sun.enterprise.server.logging.GFFileHandler.rotationTimeLimitInMinutes` allows you to rotate the logfiles (close the current file and start a new one) after a specific number of minutes to avoid the logfiles becoming unmanageably large
- `com.sun.enterprise.server.logging.GFFileHandler.rotationLimitInBytes` allows you to rotate the logfiles when they reach a specific size

Controlling individual loggers

In the last section, you find lines of the format `<class>.level=<LEVEL>`, for example, `javax.enterprise.system.level=INFO`. Add your own loggers to this section to control how much of the logging in your application you want in the logfile.

If you application has the base URL `com.company.rental`, you can add the following statement to see all log statements:

    com.company.rental.level=FINEST

You can choose any of the log levels: SEVERE, WARNING, INFO, CONFIG, FINE, FINER, or FINEST. You can also set different log levels for different loggers, for example:

    com.company.rental.level=INFO

    com.company.rental.view.beans.RentalBean.level=FINEST

This will provide INFO logging for your entire application but FINEST logging for your `RentalBean` logger.

> You can also control GlassFish logging with the `asadmin` command-line tool as described in the Oracle GlassFish Server 3.1 Administration Guide:
>
> http://docs.oracle.com/cd/E18930_01/html/821-2416/gklmn.html

Debugging in JDeveloper

As you have already noticed, deploying the application on the built-in WebLogic server is much faster than deploying it to GlassFish. That's why you'll want to develop and debug your application on WebLogic and occasionally deploy it for testing on GlassFish. In theory, your ADF Essentials application is just a JEE application like any other—so, if it runs on WebLogic, it should run on GlassFish. In practice, you'll want to make sure it does run on GlassFish.

Automated deployment

It is a good idea to develop an automated build of the application. If you combine this with a continuous integration tool like Hudson/Jenkins, you can set up an automatic build and deploy to GlassFish to run once a day. That will enable you to check that the code you develop on WebLogic can also be deployed on GlassFish. If you add some simple UI testing to your automated build script, you can even verify that your code actually runs on GlassFish.

Debugging code

In order to debug your application, you must first place one or more breakpoints in your code by left-clicking in the left margin or right-clicking and choosing **Toggle Breakpoint** as shown in the following screenshot:

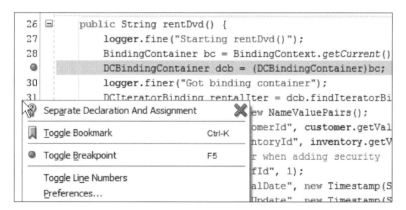

Now start your web page by right-clicking on it and choosing **Debug** (instead of **Run**). If the built-in WebLogic server is running in "regular" mode, you will be asked if you want to restart the server in "debug" mode or vice versa.

Debugging ADF Applications

 When the built-in WebLogic server is running, it is in either regular or debug mode. Your application runs faster in regular mode, so this is what you should be using during most of development. Only switch to debug mode if you need to track down complicated issues that cannot be resolved through the use of log statements alone.

Remember that you cannot run task flows based on page fragments directly. You will have to build a test page and drop your bounded task flow onto the page as a static region.

Upon reaching the breakpoint, execution stops and the cursor is placed on the code line that has the breakpoint. If your breakpoint is placed before the page is rendered to the browser, your browser will seem stuck retrieving the page. The JDeveloper toolbar and the **Run** menu contain the normal functions, listed as follows, that you expect from a debugger:

- **Step Over**
- **Step Into**
- **Step Out**
- **Step to End**
- **Resume**

The icons are placed in the JDeveloper toolbar next to the **Run/Debug/Terminate** buttons and look like this:

Additionally, you can place the cursor further down in the code, right-click, and choose **Run to Cursor** (or choose **Run to Cursor** from the **Run** menu). This can be useful, for example, when you have single-stepped through the first couple of loop iterations and want to continue debugging after the loop.

In the **Log** window, you will see several new tabs:

- The **Breakpoints** tab shows all breakpoints in the current application workspace.
- The **Smart Data** tab attempts to make an intelligent guess and shows you only the variables that JDeveloper thinks will be interesting to you at this specific point in the execution. It looks like this:

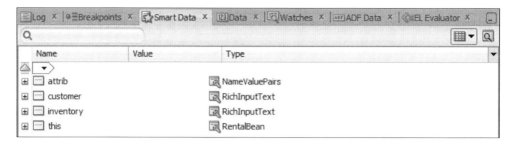

- The **Data** tab shows all variables.
- The **Watch** tab allows you to define expressions to watch. Some of the ADF business component classes are rather complicated to read on the **Data** tab, so it is often easier to set up a watch using an object and a method. Either right-click inside the **Watch** tab or right-click on a variable in the code and choose **Watch** from the context menu.
- The **ADF Data** tab shows you the values that are stored in various memory scopes.
- The **EL Evaluator** tab allows you to evaluate Expression Language expressions using the #{xxx} syntax.

Understanding the ADF lifecycle

As you gain experience with ADF development, at some point in time, you will probably want to learn about the ADF lifecycle. In all **JavaServer Faces (JSF)** applications, processing of a request that arrives at the server from a browser goes through some very specific phases. In a standard JSF application, this lifecycle includes six phases—in an ADF application, there are additional ADF-specific phases as well.

To learn about the ADF lifecycle, refer to the Oracle Fusion Middleware Web User Interface Developer's Guide for Oracle Application Development Framework. In the guide for JDeveloper 11.1.2.4.0, the lifecycle is described in *Chapter 5, Building Enterprise Applications*. You can find this at http://docs.oracle.com/cd/E37975_01/web.111240/e16181/af_lifecycle.htm.

Debugging ADF Applications

While you are debugging, you can follow the request processing through the various phases in the **Structure** panel. This panel is normally shown in the bottom-left corner of the JDeveloper window and shows the structure of whatever you have active (code classes, JSF pages, and so on) on the first tab. However, while debugging, it also shows the call stack on the **Stack** tab and the structure of the ADF page running on the **ADF Structure** tab. At the top of the **ADF Structure** tab, it also shows which ADF lifecycle phase is currently active (for example, JSF Invoke Application). The **ADF Structure** tab might look like this when your application is stopped at a breakpoint:

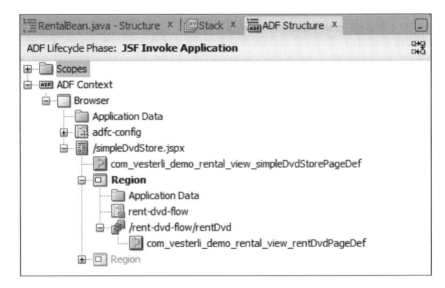

 You can click on the small button to the right of the current lifecycle phase to set a breakpoint at a specific phase. Once you have achieved a good understanding of the JSF and ADF lifecycle, this feature might be useful to you.

Debugging task flows

Sometimes, you might need to track down an issue, but you are not quite sure in which class the problem lies. In this case, you can place breakpoints in your task flows.

To place a breakpoint on any task flow activity, right-click on it and choose **Toggle Breakpoint**. This can be done on all activities, including views, method calls, and task flow invocations. A breakpoint is shown with a red dot, like the one shown in the following screenshot:

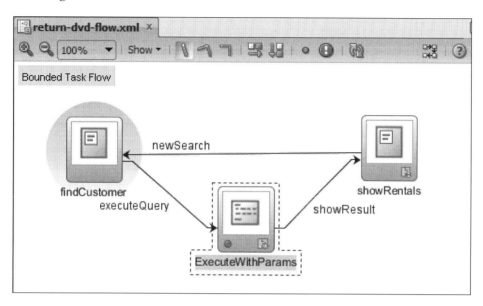

When you run your application and it stops at a breakpoint, the **Data** and **Smart Data** tabs will not show variable values because you are not actually executing any Java code at that moment. Instead, they will show an `activityBreakpointDetail` item with details about the breakpoint where execution is halted. Additionally, you can use the **EL Evaluator** tab to evaluate EL expressions. This can be useful to determine which parameters are passed into and returned from elements of the task flow.

Debugging ADF Applications

When your application stops at a task flow breakpoint, it might look like this:

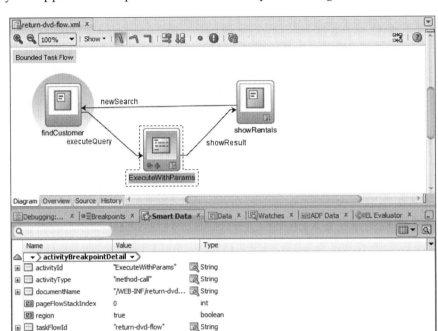

Debugging into ADF libraries

If you are building your application in a proper enterprise application structure as described in *Chapter 5, Building Enterprise Applications*, you will be using ADF libraries extensively. So, how do you follow execution into ADF libraries?

The solution is to deploy the source code of your subsystems as separate JAR files and include these source JAR files in your application. The procedure for creating a source JAR file is very similar to how you created an ADF library:

1. Create a directory to hold your source JAR files.
2. Create new deployment profiles in your subsystems and deploy them.
3. Include the source JAR files in your master project.

Creating a source directory

You can create the directory anywhere, but it is a good idea to place it in your master project. Call it something like `sourcejars` to indicate its use.

Creating a source JAR file

For each project that you want to debug into, choose **Project Properties**, **Deployment** to get to the deployment dialog. From here, click on **New** to create a new deployment profile, choose **JAR File** as **Profile Type**, and give it a name that contains your subsystem name (for example, sourceDraRentDvd). In the **JAR Deployment Profile Properties** dialog, first select the **JAR Options** node to the right and correct the content of the **JAR File** field. Initially, it will contain a path to your project deploy directory—you want to change this so the finished JAR file is placed directly in your sourcejars directory. An example of a corrected value would be C:\JDeveloper\mywork\sourcejars\sourceDraRentDvd. Now, expand **File Groups** and then **Project Output**. Under **Contributors**, make sure that only **Project Source Path** is checked, as shown in the following screenshot:

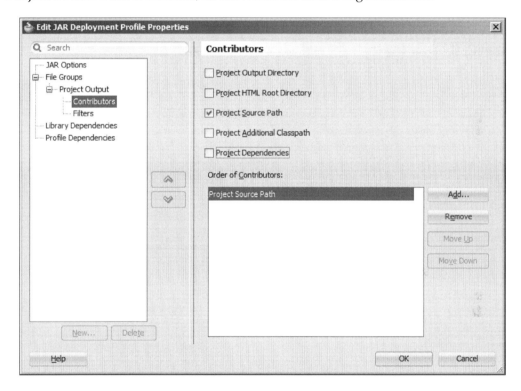

When you have created the deployment profile, you can right-click on your project and choose to deploy to the source deployment profile. This creates a JAR file in the location you specified.

Including the source in the master application

Now you need to include the source JAR file in the master application. To do this, open the master application, right-click on the master project, and choose **Project Properties | Libraries and Classpath**. Click on **Add Library** and then on **New** to create a new library. Give your source library a name that contains the project abbreviation, for example, `DraSource`. Set **Location** to **Project**. In the **Create Library** dialog, select the **Source Path** node and then click on **Add Entry**. In the **Select Path Entry** dialog, navigate to your `sourcejars` directory and select your source JAR files (you can *Ctrl* + click to select multiple files). Your dialog should look like the one shown in the following screenshot:

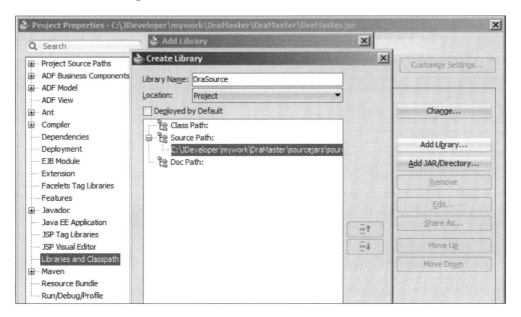

Placing a breakpoint in an ADF library

In order to set a breakpoint in an ADF library that you have attached to a project, you need to change the display options for the **Application Navigator**. In your master project, find the **Navigator Display Options** button next to **Projects** at the top of the navigator, as shown in the following screenshot:

Chapter 6

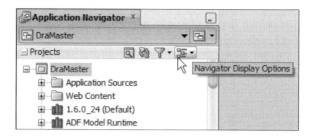

Click on the **Navigator Display Options** button and choose **Show Libraries** as shown in the following screenshot:

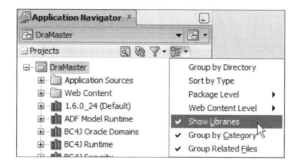

You will now see a lot of new nodes in the **Application Navigator**—all of the libraries your application is using. These are the actual JAR files that JDeveloper includes in your project as a consequence of your technology choices for the project, as well as the source JAR you added yourself.

If you scroll down, you will see the library you added (for example, DraSource), and if you click on the plus sign, you will see the combined Java package hierarchy from all of the source JAR files you included in your library. Navigate down the hierarchy to the class where you want to set the breakpoint, open it, and set the breakpoint like you would for a local class (right-click in the left margin).

Now, when you run your application in debug mode, execution will stop inside your ADF library at the breakpoint. From here, you can debug the code from the library just like local code in the project with **Step Into** | **Step Over** and the various tabs for displaying data and application state.

> While you are debugging and making changes to the code, make sure to deploy your subsystem both as an ADF library and as a source JAR. If you place a breakpoint in a source JAR file that does not correspond to the actual ADF library being executed, the cursor placement in the source code might be off.

[209]

Debugging into the ADF source code

As you are stepping through your code with **Step Into**, you will eventually reach a point where you see the dialog shown in the following screenshot:

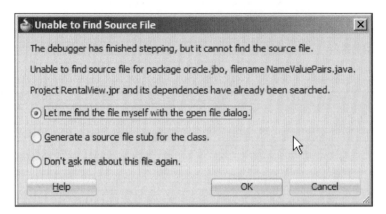

This means that code execution has moved into the ADF base classes delivered by Oracle in the ADF Essentials libraries. These libraries contain only the compiled classes, so the debugger can't show you the source code.

While ADF Essentials is free (in the "no-cost" meaning of the word), it is not open source. You can't just download the source code from OTN or elsewhere.

However, you can purchase a support contract for ADF Essentials from Oracle. At the time of writing, this price was USD 1,250 per year per server. Note the cost is per server and not per CPU as other Oracle prices. If you purchase this support contract, you get a Customer Support Identifier that entitles you to open service requests with Oracle support.

That's fine if you have an issue with a feature that doesn't work the way you expect it to or a component that misbehaves in a specific browser. But equally important is the fact that the support contract entitles you to receive a copy of the ADF source code. In order to receive it, you must open a service request requesting the source code for a specific version of ADF. You will be given some paperwork to complete that lays out the restrictions on what you can do with the code (you can't publish it, among other things). Once you have done the paperwork and returned it to Oracle, you will be given access to download the source code, normally within a couple of days.

Once you have the source code, you need to make it available to JDeveloper. This is explained in one of the ADF Essentials video demonstrations available on the Oracle Technology Network and YouTube. You can search on Google for "how to implement logging in an ADF application" or go directly to `http://www.youtube.com/watch?v=FxA2Fs0zhAM`.

Summary

You have seen how to use ADF logging and JDeveloper debugging features to find out in detail what your application is doing. With this knowledge, you should be able to ensure that your application has the required functionality.

In the next chapter, we will see how you control who can use the application by adding security to your ADF Essentials application.

7
Securing an ADF Essentials Application

You have developed the functionality of your ADF Essentials application, but you probably don't want every feature to be available to everybody. To ensure that only the right users get access to the right information, you need **authentication** (to identify the user of the application) and **authorization** (to control what each user is allowed to do).

If you are running the full version of ADF on WebLogic, the ADF framework offers a comprehensive set of security features. However, since we are running ADF Essentials on GlassFish, we will need another solution.

The Java technology stack offers the **Java Authentication and Authorization Service (JAAS)**, but this solution is rather complex and not very popular among developers. Instead, in this chapter, we will implement Apache Shiro security for our application.

Apache Shiro basics

Shiro is a project with a long history — it started life as JSecurity back in 2003 when there were really few options for Java security. It provides four main pieces of functionality:

- Authentication
- Authorization
- Cryptography
- Session management

Securing an ADF Essentials Application

We'll be using the authentication part (determining who the user is) and the authorization part (determining what the user can do). For the purposes of this book, we will not be using the cryptography (encrypting and decrypting data) or the session management (we rely on standard JSF and ADF functionality for our session data).

Getting the software

You can download the Shiro software from http://shiro.apache.org. You'll want the **Latest Stable Release, Binary Distribution**. Download the shiro-core and shiro-web JAR files.

Because you don't want your application to depend on a directory outside the application structure, create a directory called extjars in the application directory and place your JAR files there.

The Shiro code uses **Simple Logging Façade for Java (SLF4J)**, so you also need to download SLF4J from http://www.slf4j.org. Download the ZIP file, unpack it somewhere, and copy the slf4j-api-1.7.5.jar and slf4j-simple-1.7.5.jar files to the same directory. If a newer version than 1.7.5 is available by the time you read this, use that instead.

Installing the packages in your application

To use Shiro security in your application, you need to include the JAR files in your project. To do this, choose **Project Properties** for your **View** project and then **Libraries and Classpath**. Click on **Add Library** and then **New**. Give your library the name Shiro and choose **Location** as **Project**. Then select the **Class Path** node in the tree, click on **Add Entry**, and add the four JAR files. Remember to check the **Deployed by Default** checkbox as shown in the following screenshot:

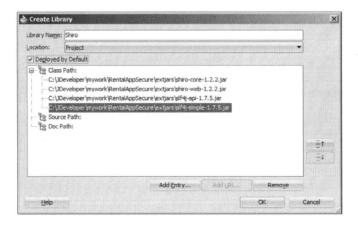

Chapter 7

The **Deployed by Default** checkbox indicates that these libraries should be deployed with the application. If you don't select this box, your application EAR file gets smaller, but you have to ensure that the libraries are available on each server you deploy it to.

Click on **OK** several times to return to the application.

Now we have the JAR files ready for use in our application, but we also need to actually configure the application to use them. So, we add a servlet filter so that every request for a page of our application is passed through Shiro. This allows Shiro to perform security evaluation before the page is shown to the user.

To add this filter, we change the `web.xml` file. You can find this file in your View project under **Web Content | WEB-INF**. When you double-click on the file, JDeveloper opens it in a specialized editor that allows you to change all settings through user-friendly dialog boxes. In this case, however, we will use the **Source** view to work directly with the file. Click on the **Source** tab at the bottom of the `web.xml` window and insert the following code:

```xml
<listener>
  <listener-class>
    org.apache.shiro.web.env.EnvironmentLoaderListener
  </listener-class>
</listener>
...
<filter>
  <filter-name>shiroFilter</filter-name>
  <filter-class>org.apache.shiro.web.servlet.ShiroFilter
    </filter-class>
</filter>
<filter-mapping>
  <filter-name>shiroFilter</filter-name>
  <url-pattern>/*</url-pattern>
  <dispatcher>REQUEST</dispatcher>
  <dispatcher>FORWARD</dispatcher>
  <dispatcher>INCLUDE</dispatcher>
  <dispatcher>ERROR</dispatcher>
</filter-mapping>
```

The `<listener>` element goes with the other `<listener>` elements, and the filter/filter-mapping block goes between the last existing `<filter>` and the first existing `<filter-mapping>`.

> The `EnvironmentLoaderListener` initializes a Shiro `WebEnvironment` instance that contains everything that Shiro needs to operate. The `ShiroFilter` instance intercepts all web requests and uses the `WebEnvironment` instance to apply security.

By placing your Shiro filter mapping first in the file, this filter is applied first at runtime. There is no need to apply the other filters if Shiro figures out that the user doesn't have access anyway.

> You can remove the `JpsFilter` (both the filter and the filter-mapping). This filter is used for **Oracle Platform Security Services** (**OPSS**), which we will not be using.

Configuring your application for Shiro

Before we secure our application, we need to know which URLs to secure. You might already have noticed that all of your pages get a URL that starts with the Java EE Web Context Root (that you can set under **Project Properties** | **Java EE Application**), followed by `/faces/`, followed by the page name. All ADF pages are rendered by the Faces servlet, so they will always have the `/faces/` part. This means that if you select to secure `/faces`, all ADF pages in your application are protected.

> The URL part `/faces/` is just a convention for JSF applications. It is defined in `web.xml`, but you can change it if you want.

Shiro is configured through the use of a Shiro INI configuration file. Create a new file (item type **File** in the **New** dialog), call it `shiro.ini`, and place it in the `/WEB-INF` directory of the **view** project.

> The `/WEB-INF` location is one of the default places Shiro looks for configuration information. You can also place the file elsewhere as long as you tell Shiro where to look for it. Refer to the Shiro documentation for information about this (`http://shiro.apache.org/web.html`).

We'll start with the simplest possible INI file:

```
[users]
user1 = welcome1

[urls]
/faces/** = authcBasic
```

Chapter 7

 This defines one user as `user1` with the password `welcome1` and secures all URLs starting with `/faces` with the `authcBasic` filter.

Deploy your application to the GlassFish server and run it. The browser will now prompt you for a username and password when you try to access any ADF page as shown in the following screenshot:

You are getting the ugly gray dialog box that is standard for the browser because the `authcBasic` instruction tells Shiro to use basic authentication. This is an old-fashioned way of doing security back from the Web Stone Age, but because it only uses features from the HTTP protocol, it is very easy to set up.

Doesn't (quite) work in WebLogic

If you don't have the patience to wait for a JDeveloper GlassFish deployment, you might be tempted to just run the application in the built-in WebLogic server. That sort of works, but because WebLogic also has security features, you'll be prompted for a username and password twice. The first time, the dialog will look as the preceding screenshot ("The site says: application") and will require a username/password from your `shiro.ini` file. The second time, the dialog asks for a WebLogic username/password, and the dialog will include "The site says: WebLogic Server". In this second dialog, you will have to provide a valid WebLogic user (for example, the administrator user, often called `weblogic`).

Advanced Shiro

Naturally, we don't want the user to be subjected to an old-fashioned browser login prompt — we want to present the user with a nice login page that matches the rest of the application. For that purpose, we need **form-based authentication**.

Additionally, we don't want our users stored in a configuration file. We could store them in an LDAP server, but that's another moving part. So, to keep it simple, we will use database tables in our existing `Sakila` connection to store our users, roles, and permissions.

There are quite a few elements and arcane Shiro incantations required to make the whole thing work. This chapter cannot describe everything in detail — refer to the Shiro documentation and the following two blog posts for more information:

- `http://balusc.blogspot.sg/2013/01/apache-shiro-is-it-ready-for-java-ee-6.html` (by Bauke Scholtz)
- `http://www.jobinesh.com/2013/02/securing-your-adf-applications-using.html` (by Jobinesh Purushothaman)

User database

Users and roles belong to **realms**, and Shiro is prepared for database authorization and authentication through the pre-built `JdbcRealm`. You can see in the documentation that this requires three queries:

- Get the password for a specific username
- Get all role names for a specific username
- Get all permissions for a specific role name

There are many ways of implementing such a security database. One example is to have tables of users, roles, and permissions like this:

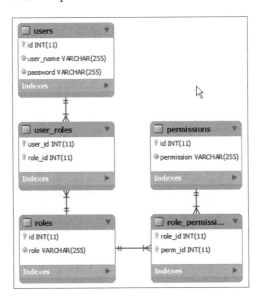

From within JDeveloper, you can open the **Database Navigator** (from the **View** menu), open the `Sakila` database connection in your application, and then run a script like the following:

```
create table users (
id int primary key auto_increment,
user_name varchar(255) unique not null,
password varchar(255) not null);

create table roles (
id int primary key auto_increment,
role varchar(255) unique not null);

create table user_roles (
user_id int not null,
role_id int not null,
foreign key (user_id) references users(id),
foreign key (role_id) references roles(id),
primary key (user_id, role_id));

create table permissions (
id int primary key auto_increment,
permission varchar(255) unique not null);

create table role_permissions (
role_id int not null,
perm_id int not null,
foreign key (role_id) references roles(id),
foreign key (perm_id) references permissions(id),
primary key (role_id, perm_id));
```

This structure allows each user to have one or more roles, and each role to be assigned to one or more users. Similarly, each role can be associated with one or more permissions, and each permission can be part of one or more roles.

Form-based authentication

If we want our own login page, we need to build it. In other contexts, it is possible to use a simple HTML-based login page with Shiro, but for an ADF application where we use JSF, we need to create a JSF login page and a backing bean to perform the actual login operations.

The page needs:

- A username field
- A password field
- A login button

The fields need to be mapped to attributes in the backing bean, and the bean also needs to provide a login method mapped to the button. Additionally, it would be nice if the bean could also offer a logout function.

The login page

Create a new JSF page called `login.jsf` (document type **Facelets**, based on your page template). Drop a **PanelFormLayout** on the page and then drop two `InputText` components on it. Place a button in the bottom facet of the **PanelFormLayout**. Set the labels, and for the password field, set the **Secret** property to **true** so that the characters you type in the password field are not shown. Your login screen should look like this:

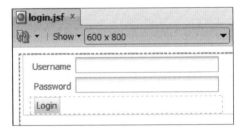

The login bean

Double-click on the **Login** button and click on **New** in the **Bind Action Property** dialog to create a new managed bean. Call it `LoginBean`, place it in a `.view.beans` package under your project root package, and choose `backingBean` as the scope. Click on **OK** and set the **Method** name to `login()`.

In the bean, we need attributes to map to the fields on the screen like you saw in *Chapter 4, Adding Business Logic*. In the code editor, create the attributes `userName` and `password` of type `String` and generate accessors. Set the **Value** property for the **Username** input text field in the login page to `#{backingBeanScope.LoginBean.userName}` and the **Value** for the **Password** field to `#{backingBeanScope.LoginBean.password}`.

The login method

Now you need to add login functionality to the `login()` method in the bean. Open the `LoginBean` class, define a `logger` object and a `HOME_URL` constant at the top, and provide content for the `login()` method:

```
...
public class LoginBean
   private ADFLogger logger =
       ADFLogger.createADFLogger(LoginBean.class);
   private final String HOME_URL = "/welcome.jsf";
...
   public String login() {
     try {
       // attempt login
       SecurityUtils.getSubject().login(
           new UsernamePasswordToken(userName, password));
       // retrieve the saved request
       HttpServletRequest request =
           (HttpServletRequest)(FacesContext.getCurrentInstance().
           getExternalContext().getRequest());
       SavedRequest savedRequest =
           WebUtils.getAndClearSavedRequest(request);
       // get external context in order to redirect
       ExternalContext externalContext =
           FacesContext.getCurrentInstance().getExternalContext();
       if (savedRequest != null) {
         logger.fine("Retrieved saved URL '" +
             savedRequest.getRequestUrl() + "', redirecting");
         externalContext.redirect(savedRequest.getRequestUrl());
       } else {
         logger.fine("No URL retrieved, redirecting to HOME_URL: "
             + HOME_URL);
         externalContext.redirect(HOME_URL);
       }
     } catch (AuthenticationException e) {
       logger.config("Failed login validation for user " +
           userName);
       FacesMessage msg =
           new FacesMessage(FacesMessage.SEVERITY_ERROR,
           "Invalid username/password combination", "");
       FacesContext.getCurrentInstance().addMessage(null, msg);
     } catch (Exception e) {
       logger.warning("Unexpected error during login", e);
     }
     return null;
   }
```

Securing an ADF Essentials Application

> The imports should resolve automatically except for a few classes that exist in more than one package. Import `SecurityUtils` from `org.apache.shiro`, `Subject` from `org.apache.shiro.subject`, and `AuthenticationException` from `org.apache.shiro.authc`.

This code uses Shiro functionality to create a new `UsernamePasswordToken` object. If login fails, this raises an `AuthenticationException` object that will show a `FacesMessage`.

If an exception is not raised, we retrieve the `HttpRequest` object and then get any saved request using `getAndClearSavedRequest()`. If we get a `SavedRequest` object, it means that the user ended up at this login page because they tried to access a protected page. In this case, we want to return the user to the originally requested page when login is successful. If we do not get a `SavedRequest` object, we send the user to the application home page defined in `HOME_URL`.

The user filter

Because Shiro was born in the classic HTML and JSP world, it doesn't really understand all the asynchronous JavaScript used in a modern JSF application. This means that we cannot use a plain Shiro `UserFilter` filter to redirect to the login page, but we instead need to build our own. Fortunately, JEE developer Bauke Scholtz has already figured out how to built such a filter, and he has documented it on his blog (http://balusc.blogspot.sg/2013/01/apache-shiro-is-it-ready-for-java-ee-6.html). The following filter is verbatim the one he developed.

Create a Java class called `FacesAjaxAwareUserFilter` in a new `view.filter` Java package under your application base package with content as follows:

> Change the following package name to your own package name. Remember which one you use—you'll refer to the fully qualified class in your `shiro.ini` file.

```
package com.adfessentials.rental.view.filter;

import java.io.IOException;
import javax.servlet.ServletRequest;
import javax.servlet.ServletResponse;
import javax.servlet.http.HttpServletRequest;
import org.apache.shiro.web.filter.authc.UserFilter;

public class FacesAjaxAwareUserFilter extends UserFilter {
  private static final String FACES_REDIRECT_XML =
```

```
   "<?xml version=\"1.0\" encoding=\"UTF-8\"?>" +
   "<partial-response><redirect " +
   "url=\"%s\"></redirect></partial-response>";

  @Override
  protected void redirectToLogin(ServletRequest req,
      ServletResponse res) throws IOException {
    HttpServletRequest request = (HttpServletRequest)req;
    if ("partial/ajax".
        equals(request.getHeader("Faces-Request"))) {
      res.setContentType("text/xml");
      res.setCharacterEncoding("UTF-8");
      res.getWriter().printf(FACES_REDIRECT_XML,
          request.getContextPath() + getLoginUrl());
    } else {
      super.redirectToLogin(req, res);
    }
  }
}
```

> This class overrides the redirectToLogin() method that is called whenever a user tries to access a protected resource without a valid session (either because they have not logged in or because their session has expired). Instead of just issuing a regular HTTP 302 redirect (that won't work with JSF), this code issues a correct JSF partial-response.

The Shiro configuration

In the shiro.ini file, we need to set up the datasource object where our users, roles, and permissions are stored, and tell Shiro which queries to use. Place the following in your shiro.ini file:

```
[main]
user = com.vesterli.view.filter.FacesAjaxAwareUserFilter
shiro.loginUrl = /faces/login.jsf
user.loginUrl = /faces/login.jsf

# DataSource config
ds = org.apache.shiro.jndi.JndiObjectFactory
ds.requiredType = javax.sql.DataSource
ds.resourceName = jdbc/SakilaDS

# JDBC realm config
jdbcRealm = org.apache.shiro.realm.jdbc.JdbcRealm
jdbcRealm.permissionsLookupEnabled = true
```

```
# Configure JDBC realm SQL queries.
jdbcRealm.authenticationQuery = SELECT password FROM sakila.users
WHERE user_name = ?
jdbcRealm.userRolesQuery = SELECT role FROM sakila.roles, sakila.user_
roles, sakila.users WHERE roles.id = user_roles.role_id and users.id =
user_roles.user_id and users.user_name = ?
jdbcRealm.permissionsQuery = SELECT permission FROM sakila.
permissions, sakila.role_permissions, sakila.roles WHERE permissions.
id = role_permissions.perm_id and roles.id = role_permissions.role_id
and roles.role = ?
jdbcRealm.dataSource = $ds

[urls]
/faces/** = user
```

Note the fully qualified name (including package) for your `FacesAjaxAwareUserFilter` class.

You can recognize that the database is configured in the `DataSource config` section and the SQL queries matching our data model are defined in another section. Refer to the documentation and the two blogs listed at the beginning of this section for more information.

Now, when you run any ADF page in your application, you will be prompted for a username and password. If you provide a valid username and password, you will be forwarded to the page you requested.

> In a production application, you don't want to store cleartext passwords. The blog by Bauke Scholtz referred to at the beginning of this section also contains information about how to encrypt the password and validate the password the user enters against this encrypted value.

Accessing the user

Once the user is authenticated, you can use the Expression Language expression `#{request.remoteUser}` to get the username of the currently logged-in user.

Implementing authorization

The preceding section shows you how to implement authentication—making sure that users are prompted for username and password. But in many cases, you want more than just knowing who your users are. This section describes how to implement authorization to limit what various users can do with the application.

Can I see some ID, please?

The simplest type of authorization is to divide the application into a public part that can be accessed by anyone and an authorized part that is only accessible to users with a valid username and password.

To implement this, you simply configure the [urls] section of the shiro.ini file. This section is evaluated in the order it is written, so you can place your publicly accessible pages first and assign the security method anon to these. This method means that everyone can access those URLs. Below your specifically public pages, place a URL pattern that secures the rest of the application. This could look like this:

```
[urls]
/faces/welcome.jsf = anon
/faces//** = user
```

Only the welcome.jsf page is accessible to everyone; everything else under /faces (that is, all your ADF pages) is covered by the user security defined previously in the shiro.ini file.

Are you a member, Sir?

If this simple approach does not meet your business requirements, you can add a role and permission-based authorization. Hard-coding role names into your application is very inflexible and hard to maintain. Instead, you should think of secured application functionality in terms of permissions and then assign these permissions to roles.

In our rental application, there would be a permission to rent a DVD and a permission to accept a return, and both of these would be assigned to the role of store clerk. The various parts of the code can check for these permissions, but you still have the flexibility to add a new role with only one of these permissions. For the discussion in this chapter, consider the following permission data:

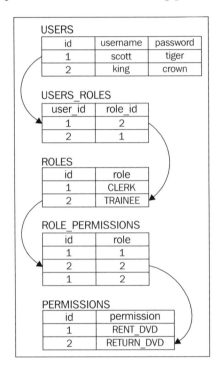

User `scott` is a TRAINEE and therefore only has RETURN_DVD permission. User `king` has role CLERK, which has both permissions RENT_DVD and RETURN_DVD.

Disabling elements

If we want to implement some authorization logic in our rental application, we can for example disable the Register rental button if the current user does not have the RENT_DVD permission.

To do this, we create the following method in our LoginBean:

```
public boolean isRentDvdAllowed() {
  Subject currentUser = SecurityUtils.getSubject();
  return currentUser.isPermitted("RENT_DVD");
}
```

This code starts by getting the Shiro Subject, which contains all the security methods we need for authorization. In this case, we return a Boolean indicating if the current user has the RENT_DVD permission. Shiro automatically looks up the user, the user's roles, and that role's permissions.

> See the Shiro documentation for more methods on Subject: http://shiro.apache.org/subject.html.

With this method programmed, we change the **Disabled** property on the Register rental button to #{!backingBeanScope.LoginBean.rentDvdAllowed}. Note the exclamation mark—the button is disabled if RENT_DVD is not allowed.

Removing elements

If you don't want to show the entire section for registering a rental, you can also find the <af:region> tag in the page and set the Rendered property:

```
<af:region value="#{bindings.rentdvdflow1.regionModel}"
  id="r1"
  rendered="#{backingBeanScope.LoginBean.rentDvdAllowed}"/>
```

In this way, the entire task flow is only rendered on the Master page if the current user has permission to rent DVDs.

Securing task flows

If you don't want to leave the security up to the user of the bounded task flow, but would like to build the security directly into the task flow itself, you can start the task flow with a method invocation and then use a Router component to stop the task flow if the user does not have access. Your task flow should look like this:

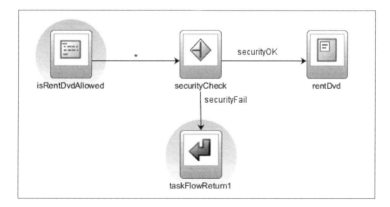

In this case, the **Default Activity** is the `isRentDvdAllowed` method call activity. The `Method` property is set to `#{backingBeanScope.LoginBean.isRentDvdAllowed}` and the `toString()` property is set to `true`. This means that a `toString()` operation is applied on the result of the method call (which returns a Boolean). The `Return Value` property is set to `#{pageFlowScope.accessAllowed}`, which means that the result (converted to a String) is stored in the `accessAllowed` variable in the page flow scope.

In the `securityCheck` **Router** component, the default outcome is set to `securityFail`, which causes an immediate return from the task flow. Additionally, one case is defined with the expression `#{pageFlowScope.accessAllowed}` (the variable where we placed the result String from the method call) and outcome `securityOK`. Your properties dialog should look like this:

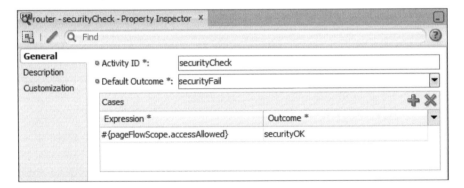

This means that only if `accessAllowed` is `true` does the flow proceed to the `rentDvd` view.

> `Router` cases must evaluate to true or false. If you want to make a decision based on a String that is not simply true or false, you have to use Expression Language operators to perform a comparison—for example, `#{pageFlowScope.operation eq 'Rental'}`.

Summary

You have now seen how to secure your ADF Essentials application with Apache Shiro so that only properly authenticated users can use your application. You have also seen several ways of using Shiro methods in beans to control access to various parts of the application.

In the last chapter, you will see how you can set up procedures to build and deploy your ADF Essentials application to test and production environments.

8
Build and Deploy

Your application is done with functionalities and the necessary security features have been applied. As you have seen many times through out the book, you can deploy your application from JDeveloper directly to the GlassFish server.

However, in a professional software development setting, you will typically want this process to be automated and not dependent on a developer having to perform a manual procedure in the development environment.

After each cycle of test and rework, you need to create a new deliverable package until it passes all tests. Then, the same package goes to the operations staff to install in the pre-production or production environment. In case your package does not install cleanly on this environment, you go back to the drawing board, fix the code or the documentation, and create a new package.

One tool for build automation is Apache Ant (http://ant.apache.org). This open source tool is included with JDeveloper (in the jdeveloper\ant subdirectory).

Creating a build script

When working with Ant, you create a buildfile (traditionally called build.xml) to specify how to build a project. This XML file consists of a number of targets that define the different goals you might want your build process to achieve, for example clean, init, compile, test, or deploy. Within each target are a number of steps called tasks. Ant comes with a large number of pre-built tasks, and many tools that integrate with Ant supply their own tasks. If you are not already familiar with Ant, there are several books and many online resources available—for example, the online manual at http://ant.apache.org/manual/index.html.

The version that is online at this URL applies to the latest version of Apache Ant—if you run the version included with JDeveloper, you are likely to be running a slightly older version.

You can run your Ant scripts from within JDeveloper by right-clicking on them and choosing either **Run Ant Target** or **Debug Ant Target**, like this:

You can also run them directly from the command line. By default, the JDeveloper subdirectory that contains Ant is not on your system path. To make it easier to use Ant, it is a good idea to add the `jdeveloper\ant\bin` directory to your PATH. Alternatively, you have to provide the whole path to the Ant executable (`C:\adfessentials\middleware111240\jdeveloper\ant\bin\ant` if you have installed in the recommended directories on Windows).

Simply change to the directory where your buildfile (`build.xml`) is placed and execute the command as follows:

ant <target>

For example:

ant deploy

Creating the script

JDeveloper can automatically generate an Ant build script for a project. To do this, simply select the project and choose **File | New**. In the **New Gallery** dialog box, change to the **All Features** tab at the top and then choose **Ant** (under **General**) and then **Buildfile from Project**, as shown in the following screenshot:

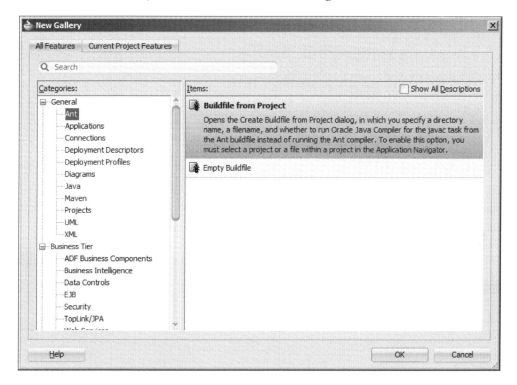

In subsystem workspaces that contain both a Model and a View project, you must create the build.xml file in the View project. Because of the dependency between the View and the Model projects (created by JDeveloper when you select **Fusion Web Application**), building the View project automatically builds the Model project).

In the following dialog box, you can leave the default filename of `build.xml`, but make sure that you check the checkbox **Include Packaging Tasks (uses ojdeploy)** as shown in the following screenshot:

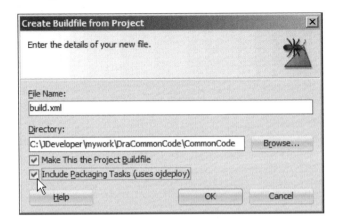

After you click on **OK**, you will see that JDeveloper has added a `build.xml` file and a `build.properties` file to your project (in the **Application Navigator**, they appear under **Resources**). You can open them to get a feel for the information they contain.

JDeveloper deployment without the user interface

The `ojdeploy` referred to by the dialog box is a command-line Java program that can do anything JDeveloper can do with regards to deployment. This program is included with JDeveloper so that you can automate your build process as described in this section. It uses some JDeveloper libraries, so it is easiest to install JDeveloper on the machine where you run it. Refer to the documentation for a thorough explanation of the many options with `ojdeploy`.

Deploying a single application

To deploy your application, you can simply right-click on the `build.xml` file. JDeveloper recognizes that the file is an Ant build file and offers special Ant menu items. Choose **Run Ant Target** and then **deploy**.

You will see a new Apache Ant subtab appearing in the log window showing the output of the Ant build process. It should end with the following line:

```
BUILD SUCCESSFUL
```

The default `build.xml` file that JDeveloper builds for you will deploy all the deployment profiles defined for the project. So, if you have a deployment profile for creating an ADF Library defined in your project, your ADF library gets built. Unless you have deleted the default deployment profile, you will see that other files (JAR or WAR) might get built as well. To avoid this, remove any superfluous deployment profiles from the project properties.

You will find the finished ADF library in the position indicated by the deployment profile—typically a `deploy` subdirectory under the project.

Building the master application

The build files in the various subsystems in your application each build only one ADF Library. However, the master application must be an EAR file containing all the ADF libraries plus the master application itself. The tasks involved include:

1. Calling all the common and subsystem workspaces in the right order to build all the ADF libraries.
2. Copying the newly built ADF libraries to a common directory (for example, in the master application).
3. Building the master application.

Starting point

Before you generate the `build.xml` file for the master application, you need to make sure that:

- Your master application project has a deployment profile that deploys the project as a WAR file
- Your master application itself has a deployment profile that deploys the application as an EAR file

When you have this, you create a `build.xml` file for the master application like you do for the subsystems. By default, this one has a `deploy` target that builds the project.

Building the application EAR file

In order to create the complete application (the EAR file), you can open the `build.xml` file and copy the entire deploy task (the tag starting `<target name="deploy"` ... until the `</target>` tag). The original deploy task builds the project—in order to make the copy build the application instead, you need to:

- Change the target name
- Add a dependency on the original deploy task
- Remove the project parameter
- Change the `outputfile` parameter

Your new task might look like this in the `build.xml` file:

```
<target name="buildear"
    description="Deploy JDeveloper profiles" depends="deploy">
  <taskdef name="ojdeploy"
      classname="oracle.jdeveloper.deploy.ant.OJDeployAntTask"
      uri="oraclelib:OJDeployAntTask"
      classpath="${oracle.jdeveloper.ant.library}"/>
    <ora:ojdeploy xmlns:ora="oraclelib:OJDeployAntTask"
        executable="${oracle.jdeveloper.ojdeploy.path}"
        ora:buildscript=
        "${oracle.jdeveloper.deploy.dir}/ojdeploy-build.xml"
        ora:statuslog=
        "${oracle.jdeveloper.deploy.dir}/ojdeploy-statuslog.xml">
      <ora:deploy>
      <ora:parameter name="workspace"
          value="${oracle.jdeveloper.workspace.path}"/>
        <ora:parameter name="profile"
            value="${oracle.jdeveloper.deploy.profile.name}"/>
        <ora:parameter name="nocompile" value="false"/>
        <ora:parameter name="outputfile" value=
        "oracle.jdeveloper.deploy.outputfile=
  C\:\\JDeveloper\\mywork\\DraMaster\\deploy\\DraMaster.ear"/>
      </ora:deploy>
    </ora:ojdeploy>
</target>
```

When you run this task, you will find that the EAR file is built with the filename and directory indicated in the `outputfile` parameter (`C:\JDeveloper\mywork\DraMaster\deploy\DraMaster.ear`).

Note that the `ojdeploy` task, despite the name, does not actually deploy the application to any application server—it merely builds all the deployment profiles.

Building all the subsystems

If you have created `build.xml` files in all your subsystems, it is easy to just call these buildfiles from your master application buildfile using an `<ant>` task.

Remember that we have three common workspaces (CommonCode, CommonModel, and CommonUI), a number of subsystems, and one master application. For the DVD Rental Application with the abbreviation `Dra`, the dependencies look like this:

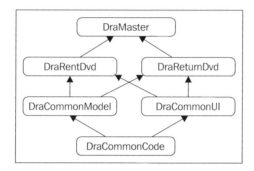

In your master buildfile, you can create a new target to build all the subsystems like this:

```
<target name="buildsub"
  description="Build common and subsystems" depends="init">
  <ant dir="${basedir}/../../DraCommonCode/CommonCode"
    inheritall="false"/>
  <ant dir="${basedir}/../../DraCommonModel/CommonModel"
    inheritall="false"/>
  <ant dir="${basedir}/../../DraCommonUI/CommonUI"
    inheritall="false"/>
  <ant dir="${basedir}/../../DraRentDvd/RentDvdView"
    inheritall="false"/>
  <ant dir="${basedir}/../../DraReturnDvd/ReturnDvdView"
    inheritall="false"/>
</target>
```

Notice that we start from the `${basedir}` location, which is where our master buildfile runs. From there, we go up two levels and then down into the individual subsystems and down into the relevant project in each subsystem to find the local `build.xml` file. You need the `inheritall=false` parameter to prevent the variable values from the master buildfile from being inherited by the subsystem build files.

When you run this task, the ADF libraries in all subsystems are built. This means that a new ADF Library is built in the `deploy` subdirectory of every project.

Copying all ADF libraries

Your build/deployment manager will normally ensure that some kind of quality assurance is performed on the ADF libraries from the subsystems before they are released to everyone else. However, if you just want to copy the libraries from each subsystem to the `adfjars` directory in your master application, you can use the Ant `<copy>` task for this.

In your master buildfile, you can create a new target to copy all ADF libraries to the master application like this:

```xml
<target name="copysub"
    description="Copy command and subsystem ADF Libraries"
    depends="init">
  <copy
      file="${basedir}/../../DraCommonCode/CommonCode/
      deploy/adflibDraCommonCode.jar"
      todir="${basedir}/../adfjars"/>
  <copy
      file="${basedir}/../../DraCommonModel/CommonModel/
      deploy/adflibDraCommonModel.jar"
      todir="${basedir}/../adfjars"/>
  <copy
      file="${basedir}/../../DraCommonUI/CommonUI/
      deploy/adflibDraCommonUI.jar"
      todir="${basedir}/../adfjars"/>
  <copy file="${basedir}/../../DraRentDvd/RentDvdView/
      deploy/adflibDraRentDvd.jar"
      todir="${basedir}/../adfjars"/>
  <copy file="${basedir}/../../DraReturnDvd/ReturnDvdView/
      deploy/adflibDraReturnDvd.jar"
      todir="${basedir}/../adfjars"/>
</target>
```

Again, we start from the `${basedir}` location and go up two levels. We then go down into the individual subsystems, and down into the relevant project in the subsystem, then going down into the `deploy` directory where the ADF Library resides. Because the line length in this book is limited, the `file` parameter is wrapped on two lines—this should be one line in your `build.xml` file.

When you run this task, all the ADF libraries from the subsystems (that were built by the `buildsub` task) are copied to the master application.

Putting it all together

Now you have all the tasks necessary to build the entire application. To make everything happen in the right order, you can change the dependencies so that `buildear` depends on `copysub` and `deploy`, and `copysub` depends on `buildsup`, like this:

```
<target name="buildear" … depends="copysub,deploy">
…
<target name="copysub" … depends="buildsub">
…
<target name="buildsub" … >
```

When you ask Ant to run the `buildear` task, it will first try to run `copysub`. However, because `copysub` depends on `buildsub`, the `buildsub` tasks runs first. Then comes `copysub`, and finally `deploy` (which builds the master project). Then, the content of the `buildear` task is run, building the actual EAR file.

Automated deployment to GlassFish

The Ant scripts described in the previous section create a **Java Enterprise Archive** (**EAR**) file, which is a complete application. The next step is to deploy it to the GlassFish server in order to be able to run it from a browser.

You have seen earlier how to create a GlassFish connection from JDeveloper and use this connection to deploy your application directly from JDeveloper to GlassFish. You can also use the GlassFish administration console at `http://<server>:<admin_port>` (for example, `http://localhost:4848`) to upload and deploy the EAR file. However, for an automated process, you need a scriptable (command-line) tool that can perform this deployment. For GlassFish, the tool that comes with the server is **asadmin**.

 You can find this tool in your GlassFish installation in the `bin` directory (if you have used the recommended directories in this book, in `C:\adfessentials\glassfish3\glassfish\bin`).

Deploying from the command line

To deploy an EAR file from the command line, simply change to the directory where your EAR file is placed and execute the following command:

`asadmin deploy <earfile>`

For the DVD Rental app, the instruction would be as follows:

`asadmin deploy DraMaster.ear`

To undeploy, the command is as follows:

`asadmin undeploy <application name>`

For example:

`asadmin undeploy DraMaster`

> Note that the `deploy` command takes a **file name** as a parameter and the `undeploy` command takes an **application name**. You set the application name under the application properties in JDeveloper.

If you are running an automated build tool like Hudson/Jenkins, you can integrate this command directly into your build tool.

Deploying from Ant

You can also run these commands from Ant with `<exec>` tasks. An example of an Ant target for undeploying is as follows:

```
<target name="undeployapp">
  <exec dir="c:\glassfish3\glassfish\bin" executable="cmd">
    <arg value="/c"/>
    <arg value="asadmin.bat"/>
    <arg value="undeploy"/>
    <arg value="DraMaster"/>
  </exec>
</target>
```

Because the `asadmin` command is a `.bat` file under Windows, you have to run the `cmd` executable with the `/c` parameter followed by the actual `.bat` filename and the parameters.

Your deploy target would therefore look like this:

```
<target name="deployapp">
  <exec dir="${basedir}/../deploy" executable="cmd">
    <arg value="/c"/>
    <arg value="c:\glassfish3\glassfish\bin\asadmin.bat"/>
    <arg value="deploy"/>
    <arg value="DraMaster.ear"/>
  </exec>
</target>
```

Integrating other functionality in your build

If you want your build and deployment procedure to run automatically, you will typically use a continuous integration tool like Hudson (http://www.hudson-ci.org). This tool can run standalone, but you can also install it into your GlassFish server.

These tools support automatically checking out the latest version of your code from source control and running tasks (like the Ant scripts in this chapter). You can define triggers (for example, build automatically after every commit to Subversion) and add additional functionality like automatic unit tests.

Preparing to go live

You can use this build procedure both during development and when you prepare to release your application. However, before you go live, you should clean up the code and set the application parameters for production use.

Cleaning up your code

Some things that you should check for in your code are:

- Database connections
- Deployment platforms
- Print statements

Additionally, JDeveloper contains a code audit tool. To see what JDeveloper thinks about your code, select a project and choose **Build | Audit**. In the **Audit** dialog box, you can click on **Edit** to select which rules you want to check in your project.

Database connections

In each subsystem where you create Business Components, you define a database connection. Hopefully, you have remembered to deploy **Connection Name Only** in all your subsystem deployment profiles as shown in the following screenshot:

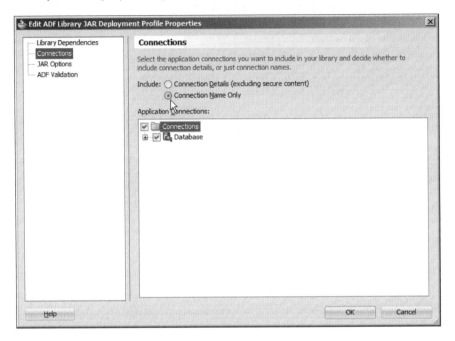

It's a good idea to check all of these before you release your application to pre-production or production environments.

Also, make sure that your installation instructions contain the name of the database connection that must exist on the server.

Deployment platforms

In the WAR deployment profile in your master application project and in the application deployment profile, remember to set **Default Platform** to **Glassfish 3.1** as shown in the following screenshot:

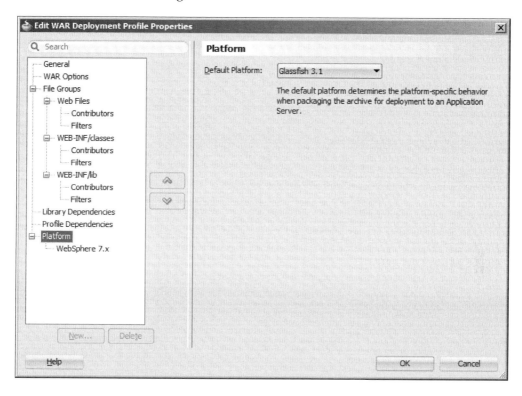

If you forget this, you might get hard-to-interpret error messages during deployment.

Print statements

Of course, you have used the logging method you all agreed on in the project team and did not write any simple `System.out.println()` statements in your code. However, somebody else might have done so. To check for these kind of impurities in your project code, you can use JDeveloper's global file search capability. Choose **Search | Find in Files** to search through your active project or application (or any user-defined path in the filesystem).

Tuning your ADF application

There are a lot of tuning parameters to tweak to make your ADF application run as fast as possible using as few resources as possible. The defaults are generally OK, but if you want to know what your options are, refer to the chapter on Oracle Application Development Framework Performance Tuning in *Oracle Fusion Middleware Performance and Tuning Guide*. Additionally, a lot of material on ADF tuning is available on the Oracle Technology Network and elsewhere on the Internet—Google oracle adf tuning for more.

Summary

Well, that's all there is to it! If you have followed the exercises in this book, you are ready to build real-world ADF Essentials applications and can consider yourself an ADF Essentials journeyman.

> A **journeyman** is someone who has completed an apprenticeship and is fully educated in a trade or craft, but not yet a master.
>
> Wikipedia, `https://en.wikipedia.org/wiki/Journeyman`, June 2013.

To continue your journey towards becoming an ADF Master, many resources are available—see the book website at `http://adfessentials.com` for some pointers as to where you could go next.

Have fun!

Index

Symbols

\<listener> element 215

A

accessors
  overriding 122-124, 131, 132
ADF application
  layers 49
  tuning 242
ADF Business Components (ADF BC)
  about 49, 50
  application modules 52
  associations 52
  entity objects 51
  view links 52
  view objects 52
  working 53, 55
ADF domain 62
ADF Essentials
  about 30, 31
  ADF Share libraries, installing in GlassFish 28
  downloading 27, 28
  GlassFish JVM parameters, setting 29, 30
  installing 27
ADF Essentials application
  application module configuration 44
  building 36
  Business Service layer 36
  business services, building 38-40
  Controller layer 36, 42
  creating 36, 37
  Database layer 36
  deploying 43
  deployment profile properties 44
  Model layer 36, 41
  MySQL Sakila demo database 38
  platform, changing 44
  running 45-48
  securing 213
  View layer 36, 42, 43
ADF libraries
  breakpoint, placing 208, 209
  creating 162, 163
  debugging into 206
  releasing 163
  source directory, creating 206
  source, including in master application 208
  source JAR file, creating 207
  using 164
  working with 162
ADF library, Common Code Workspace
  creating 171
  releasing 172
ADF library, CommonModel workspace
  adding 176, 178
ADF library, CommonUI workspace
  adding 174, 175
  creating 175
  releasing 176
ADF library folder, master application workspace
  creating 168, 169
ADF library, RentDvd subsystem workspace
  adding 178
ADF library, ReturnDvd subsystem workspace
  adding 183
ADF lifecycle 203

ADFLogger 191
ADFLogger.createADFLogger() method 192
ADF logging
  about 191
  business logging 194
  JDeveloper shortcuts 194-196
  logger, creating 192
  logs, reading 197, 198
  log statements, adding 192, 193
ADF Naming and Project Layout Guidelines
  URL 53
ADF Share libraries
  installing, in GlassFish 28
ADF source code
  debugging into 210
Advanced Shiro
  about 217, 218
  form-based authentication 219
  user, accessing 224
  user database 218, 219
Apache Ant
  URL 229
application
  deploying 232, 233
  preparing, for release 239-242
  Shiro security, using 214, 215
application module 52, 79-81
application module, RentDvd subsystem workspace
  creating 180, 181
application module, ReturnDvd subsystem workspace
  creating 185, 186
application modules, logic 134
asadmin 237
associations
  about 52
  cleaning up 66
attribute values
  working with 138, 139
authentication
  about 213
  elements, disabling 226, 227
  elements, removing 227
  task flows, securing 227, 228
authorization
  about 213
  implementing 225, 226
autogenerated values 63
automated deployment, Glassfish
  about 237
  deploying, from Ant 238
  EAR file, deploying from command line 238

B

bean
  adding, to task flow 136
  creating 142, 143, 148
  UI components, accessing from 137
bean method
  adding, to button 135, 136
binding layer
  accessing 138
binding layer, accessing
  attribute values 138, 139
  operations 139
  whole data sets 140
binding, RentDvd subsystem workspace
  adding 181, 182
bindings
  establishing 144, 145
bind variable 73
bounded task flow 86
build script
  creating 229-232
business components
  logic, adding to 121
  testing 82, 83
Business Components from Tables wizard
  running 61
business logging 194
business logic, RentDvd subsystem workspace
  adding 182
business service layer
  about 49
  possibilities 49
button
  bean method, adding to 135, 136

C

client interface 121
code
  structuring 157
code template feature 194
command line
  EAR file, deploying from 238
CommonCode Workspace
  about 159, 169
  ADF library, creating 171
  ADF library, releasing 172
  adding, to source control 170
  creating 169
  framework extension classes, re-creating 169
  JDeveloper preferences, verifying 170
CommonModel workspace
  about 159, 176
  adding, to source control 177
  ADF library, adding 176
  ADF library, creating 177
  creating 176
  entity objects, creating 176, 177
CommonUI workspace
  about 159, 172
  adding, to source control 175
  ADF library, adding 174, 175
  ADF library, creating 175
  creating 172
  releasing 176
  task flow template, creating 172, 174
conditional formatting 152
Controller layer 85
Customer Search Page Fragment, ReturnDvd subsystem workspace
  creating 187
customer view object
  building 72-75
Customer view object, ReturnDvd subsystem workspace
  creating 183

D

database triggers
  working with 124, 125

data bindings
  customer, displaying on page 113-116
  customer rentals, displaying on page 116, 117-119
  navigation, adding 120
  using 113
Data Manipulation Language (DML) 125
DataSource
  adding, in GlassFish 25, 26
data types
  cleaning up 64, 65
data validation
  about 127
  declarative validation 127, 128
  Groovy scripts 130
  method validation 130
  regular expression validation 129
declarative validation 127, 128
default activity 91
deploy command 238
doDML() method
  about 123, 125
  overriding 125, 126
domain logging
  controlling 200
domains
  about 62
  ADF domain 62
  Enum domain 63
  Mediumint domain 63
  Set domain 63
  Text domain 63
  Year domain 63
DVD rental application
  rental, registering 142
  return, registering 147

E

EAR file
  building, for application 234
  deploying, from command line 238
elements, task flow
  router 98
  task flow call 98
  task flow return 98

enterprise applications
 building 157
entity objects
 about 51
 building, for example application 59-61
 invalid references, removing from 70
entity objects, CommonModel workspace
 creating 176, 177
entity objects, logic
 about 122
 accessors, overriding 122-124
 database triggers 124, 125
 doDML() method, overriding 125, 126
Enum domain 63
example application
 associations, cleaning up 66
 autogenerated values 63
 data types, cleaning up 64, 65
 DVD rental application 141
 entity objects, building for 59-61
 labels, setting 63
 starting 53
example application, pages
 ADF query panel 109
 customer search page,
  building 106-108
 master page, building 110, 111
 page, running 112
 Rent DVD page, building 109
 Return DVD page, building 109
example application, task flow
 Rent DVD task flow, building 89-91
 Return DVD task flow, building 92-96

F

fields
 mapping 143
form-based authentication
 about 217, 219
 login bean 220
 login method 221, 222
 login page 220
 user filter 222, 223
framework extension classes
 about 56
 creating 57, 58
 using 58, 59
**framework extension classes, Common
  Code Workspace**
 re-creating 169
Full ADF
 about 30
 ADF Desktop Integration 31
 ADF Mobile 31
 ADF remote taskflows 31
 ADF Security 31
 MetaData Services 31
functionalities, Shiro 213

G

getSelectedRowKeys() method 152
GIT 160
GlassFish
 about 21
 automated deployment 237
 DataSource, adding 25, 26
 domain, setting up 23, 24
 downloading 21
 installing 21, 22
 MySQL connector, installing 25
GlassFish JVM parameters
 setting 29, 30
GlassFish logging
 about 199
 domain logging, controlling 200
 individual loggers, controlling 200
GlassFish Server Extension
 installing, in JDeveloper 33, 34
Groovy 130
Groovy scripts 130

H

Hudson
 URL 239

I

individual loggers
 controlling 200
installation
 ADF Essentials 27
 JDeveloper 30

JDK 7 19
MySQL 10
invalid references
  removing, from entity objects 70
items, returning
  attribute return value, coding 153
  attribute value, using 154
  new attribute, binding 153
  transient attribute, creating 152
iterator 140

J

Java Authentication and Authorization Service (JAAS) 213
JavaServer Faces (JSF) 203
JDeveloper
  11*g* Release 1 branch 31
  11*g* Release 2 branch 31
  about 158
  code, debugging 201-203
  debugging concepts 201
  debugging, into ADF libraries 206
  debugging, into ADF source code 210
  downloading 32
  GlassFish Server, connecting to 35
  GlassFish Server Extension,
    installing 33, 34
  installing 30, 32
  MySQL Connector, installing 32, 33
  task flows, debugging 204, 205
JDeveloper deployment
  without user interface 232
JDeveloper preferences, Common Code Workspace
  verifying 170
JDeveloper shortcuts 194-196
JDK 7
  downloading 19
  installing 19-21

L

labels
  setting, for example application 63

log4j 191
Logback 191
logger
  creating 192
logging
  persistent loggers 198
  transient loggers 198
logging guidelines
  example 193
logging.xml file 198
logic
  adding, to business components 121
  adding, to user interface 135
  in application modules 134
  in entity objects 122
  in view objects 130
logic, in business components
  about 121
  application modules 134
  data validation 127
  entity objects 122
  view objects 130
logic, user interface
  about 135
  bean, adding to task flow 136
  bean method, adding to bean 135, 136
  binding layer, accessing 138
  messages, displaying 140, 141
  UI components, accessing from beans 137
login bean, form-based authentication 220
login method, form-based authentication 221, 222
login page, form-based authentication 220
log level
  CONFIG 193
  FINE 193
  FINER 193
  FINEST 193
  INFO 193
  SEVERE 193
  WARNING 193
logs
  reading 197, 198
log statements
  adding 192, 193

M

master application
  ADF libraries, copying 236, 237
  building 233
  EAR file, building 234
  subsystems, building 235, 236
master application workspace
  about 165
  adding, to source control 166-168
  ADF libraries, adding 189
  ADF library folder, creating 168, 169
  creating 165, 166
  finishing 189
  master page, creating 189, 190
Master Workspace 159
Mediumint domain 63
memory scopes, task flow
  about 97
  BackingBean scope 97
  PageFlow scope 97
  Session scope 97
message tokens 128
method validation 130
Model layer 85
Model project 158
Model-view-controller (MVC) pattern 138
MySQL
  download link 10
MySQL connector
  installing, in GlassFish 25
  installing, in JDeveloper 32
MySQL installation
  data, modifying 18
  MySQL options, changing 16
  MySQL Workbench, starting 16-18
  performing 10-12
  server configuration 14, 15

O

operations
  working with 139
Oracle Application Development Framework (Oracle ADF) 9
Oracle Diagnostics Logging (ODL) 191
Oracle Platform Security Services (OPSS) 216

P

packages
  installing, in application 214, 215
page, bounded task flow 87
page fragment, bounded task flow 87
page fragment, RentDvd subsystem workspace
  creating 181
pages
  building 99
  building, templates used 99
pages, building
  example application 106
  facet, defining 100
  page fragment template 100-102
  page template 102-104
partial page rendering 88
persistent loggers 198
Plain Old Java Objects (POJOs) 50
prepareSession() method 134
projects 158

R

realms 218
redirectToLogin() method 223
registerReturn() method 151
regular expression validation 129
rental, DVD rental application
  registering 142
rental registration, DVD rental application
  bean, creating 142, 143
  bindings, establishing 144, 145
  code, writing 146, 147
  fields, mapping 143
Rentals Page Fragment, ReturnDvd subsystem workspace
  creating 188
rental view object
  building 75-77
Rental view object, ReturnDvd subsystem workspace
  creating 184, 185
RentDvd subsystem workspace
  about 178
  ADF library, adding 178
  application module, creating 180, 181

binding, creating 181, 182
business logic, adding 182
creating 178
page fragment, creating 181
task flow, creating 181
view object, creating 179, 180
Rent DVD task flow
building 89-91
return, DVD rental application
registering 147
ReturnDvd subsystem workspace
about 182
ADF libraries, adding 183
application module, creating 185, 186
creating 183
Customer Search Page Fragment, creating 187
Customer view object, creating 183
Rentals Page Fragment, creating 188
rental view object, creating 184, 185
return, registering 188
task flow, creating 187
View Link, creating 185
Return DVD task flow
building 92-96
return registration, DVD rental application
bean code, writing 151
bean, creating 148
bindings, establishing 151
button, adding 147
column, adding 147
method, publishing 150
table, mapping 148
view object method, creating 149
return, ReturnDvd subsystem workspace
registering 188

S

Set domain 63
setLastName() method 124
setOverdueDayLimit() method 133
Shiro
about 213
application 216, 217
functionalities 213
packages, installing in application 214, 215
URL, for downloading 214
Shiro configuration 223, 224
Shiro INI configuration file 216
shiro.ini file 223
Shiro security
using, in application 214, 215
Simple Logging Façade for Java (SLF4J)
about 214
URL 214
source control
adding, to Common Code Workspace 170
adding, to CommonModel workspace 178
adding, to CommonUI workspace 175
adding, to master application workspace 166-168
SQL injection 74
SQL statements
logging 199
storyboard 71, 72
Subsystem Workspaces 159
superfluous associations
deleting 67, 68

T

table
mapping 148
task flow, RentDvd subsystem workspace
creating 181
task flow, ReturnDvd subsystem workspace
creating 187
task flows
bean, adding to 136
bounded task flow 86
building 86
debugging 204, 205
elements 98
example application 89
memory scopes 97
page fragment 87
pages 87
securing 227, 228
task flow templates 88, 89
unbounded task flow 86
task flow template, CommonUI workspace
creating 173, 174
task flow templates

[249]

about 88
building 88, 89
Text domain 63
transient attribute 152
transient loggers 198

U

UI components
　accessing, from beans 137
unbounded task flow 86
undeploy command 238
user, Advanced Shiro
　accessing 224
user database, Advanced Shiro 218, 219
user filter, form-based authentication 222, 223

V

version control
　outside JDeveloper 162
　using 160, 161
view criteria
　about 52
　modifying 132, 133
view criterion 183
View layer 85
view link
　creating 78, 79
View Link, ReturnDvd subsystem workspace
　creating 185
View Links 52
view object method
　creating 149

view object, RentDvd subsystem workspace
　creating 179, 180
view objects
　about 52
　building 71
　customer view object, building 72-75
　rental view object, building 75-77
　storyboard 71, 72
　view link, creating 78, 79
view objects, logic
　about 130
　accessors, overriding 131, 132
　view criteria, modifying 132, 133
View project 158

W

WebLogic
　DataSource, adding to 47, 48
　setting up, for MySQL 47
whole data sets
　working with 140
workspace 158
workspace hierarchy 158, 159
wrong associations
　fixing 68, 69

Thank you for buying
Developing Web Applications with Oracle ADF Essentials

About Packt Publishing

Packt, pronounced 'packed', published its first book "Mastering phpMyAdmin for Effective MySQL Management" in April 2004 and subsequently continued to specialize in publishing highly focused books on specific technologies and solutions.

Our books and publications share the experiences of your fellow IT professionals in adapting and customizing today's systems, applications, and frameworks. Our solution based books give you the knowledge and power to customize the software and technologies you're using to get the job done. Packt books are more specific and less general than the IT books you have seen in the past. Our unique business model allows us to bring you more focused information, giving you more of what you need to know, and less of what you don't.

Packt is a modern, yet unique publishing company, which focuses on producing quality, cutting-edge books for communities of developers, administrators, and newbies alike. For more information, please visit our website: www.packtpub.com.

About Packt Enterprise

In 2010, Packt launched two new brands, Packt Enterprise and Packt Open Source, in order to continue its focus on specialization. This book is part of the Packt Enterprise brand, home to books published on enterprise software – software created by major vendors, including (but not limited to) IBM, Microsoft and Oracle, often for use in other corporations. Its titles will offer information relevant to a range of users of this software, including administrators, developers, architects, and end users.

Writing for Packt

We welcome all inquiries from people who are interested in authoring. Book proposals should be sent to author@packtpub.com. If your book idea is still at an early stage and you would like to discuss it first before writing a formal book proposal, contact us; one of our commissioning editors will get in touch with you.

We're not just looking for published authors; if you have strong technical skills but no writing experience, our experienced editors can help you develop a writing career, or simply get some additional reward for your expertise.

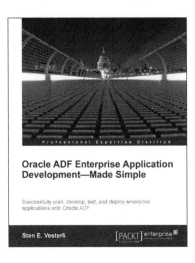

Oracle ADF Enterprise Application Development—Made Simple

ISBN: 978-1-84968-188-9 Paperback: 396 pages

Successfully plan, develop, test, and deploy enerprise applications with Oracle ADF

1. Best practices for real-life enterprise application development
2. Proven project methodology to ensure success with your ADF project from an Oracle ACE Director
3. Understand the effort involved in building an ADF application from scratch, or converting an existing application

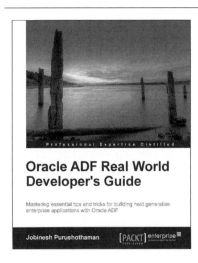

Oracle ADF Real World Developer's Guide

ISBN: 978-1-84968-482-8 Paperback: 590 pages

Mastering essential tips and tricks for building next gernation enterprise application with Oracle ADF

1. Full of illustrations, diagrams, and tips with clear step-by-step instructions and real-time examples
2. Get to know the visual and declarative programming model offered by ADF.
3. In depth coverage of ADF business components and ADF binding layer
4. Teaches you the ADF best practices and fine-tuning tips

Please check www.PacktPub.com for information on our titles

Oracle ADF 11gR2 Development Beginner's Guide

ISBN: 978-1-84968-900-7   Paperback: 330 pages

Experience the easiest way to learn, understand, and implement rich Internet application using Oracle ADF 11gR2

1. Implement a web-based application using the powerful ADF development framework from Oracle

2. Experience the fun of building a simple web application with practical examples and step-by-step instructions

3. Understand the power of Oracle ADF 11gR2 and develop any complex application with confidence

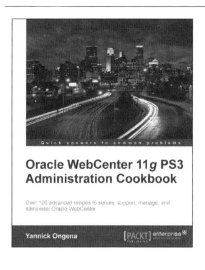

Oracle WebCenter 11g PS3 Administration Cookbook

ISBN: 978-1-84968-228-2   Paperback: 348 pages

A J2EE developer's guide to using Oracle JDeveloper's integrated database features to build data-driven applications

1. The only book and eBook in the market that focuses on administration tasks using the new features of WebCenter 11g PS3

2. Understand the use of Wiki and Discussion services to build collaborative portals

3. Full of illustrations, diagrams, and tips with clear step-by-step instructions and real-world examples

4. Learn how to build rich enterprise 2.0 portals with WebCenter 11g

Please check **www.PacktPub.com** for information on our titles

Printed in Germany
by Amazon Distribution
GmbH, Leipzig